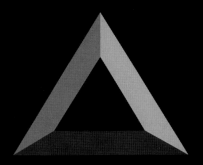

The Rich Barber®

THE
RICH
BARBER
METHOD

HOW TO ATTRACT CLIENTS, KEEP THEM, AND CHARGE MORE

CHUKA TORRES

This book has free bonus material, digital tools, and training that go along with it. To get access, go here now and start implementing what you are learning.

TheRichBarberMethod.com

Book design by Bobby Birchall (bobbyandco.com)
Book edited and produced by Joshua Raab (joshuaraab.com)

Photos on pages 2, 17, 24,101,107,122 , and the cover photo are by Common Space Media.

Although the author and publisher have made every effort to ensure that the information in this book was correct at press time, the author and publisher do not assume and hereby disclaim any liability to any party for any loss, damage, or disruption caused by errors or omissions, whether such errors or omissions result from negligence, accident, or any other cause. Some names and identifying details have been changed to protect the privacy of individuals.

Andis, Wahl, Oster, Bevel, and BabyBliss Pro products and titles are registered trademarks of their respective companies.

To my daughter Amirah,
I love you so much!

Since the day you were born
you have been the sweetest
most loving girl in the world.

Thank you.

THE RICH BARBER METHOD

DEVELOPMENTAL PYRAMID

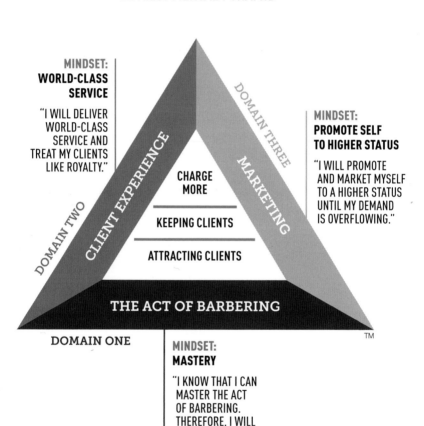

MINDSET:
WORLD-CLASS SERVICE

"I WILL DELIVER WORLD-CLASS SERVICE AND TREAT MY CLIENTS LIKE ROYALTY."

MINDSET:
PROMOTE SELF TO HIGHER STATUS

"I WILL PROMOTE AND MARKET MYSELF TO A HIGHER STATUS UNTIL MY DEMAND IS OVERFLOWING."

DOMAIN THREE
MARKETING

CLIENT EXPERIENCE

DOMAIN TWO

CHARGE MORE

KEEPING CLIENTS

ATTRACTING CLIENTS

THE ACT OF BARBERING

DOMAIN ONE

TM

MINDSET:
MASTERY

"I KNOW THAT I CAN MASTER THE ACT OF BARBERING. THEREFORE, I WILL THINK MASTERY AND STRIVE TO ACHIEVE MASTERY OF MY CRAFT DAILY."

TABLE OF CONTENTS

What You're About to Master: The Billion Dollar Barber Industry

In 2017, Forbes published an article that claimed barbering was the fastest growing profession in the United States and projected it would be a $26 billion dollar industry by 2020.

WTF! Pause and really think about that.

Other than hieroglyphics I've seen of ancient Egyptians getting their kin poppin' with the clippers, there has never been a better time in history to leverage your passion as a barber. Today, barbers have access to social media, marketing, and business tools that they can leverage to build strong and stable lives for themselves and their families. That's why I couldn't let 2018 pass by without giving you The Rich Barber Method.

To find your labor of love and maximize your earning potential is a wonderful thing that very few people get to do and experience. You can do both.

Our work can make a meaningful impact on the world. Cut by cut, we distribute self-confidence and change the way someone feels about themselves. And now, because the way someone looks is something they share online and get instant feedback on, the barber's impact is powerful in a whole new way. The more I observe our industry, the more I see its penetration and influence on nearly every aspect of modern society. It's doing this in a very similar way hip-hop culture has.

This is our labor of love, and the opportunity it presents is abundant. It's given me everything I asked for, and because you picked up this book, it's an indication that it's time for you to get everything you ask for.

This book was written to help barbers build as strong a foundation as possible for their careers. It is organized in such a way that it will not only bring growth to your career, but also to your character. When you finish this book, you'll find you have a changed perspective on your life and your future.

All of these lessons are based on real-life experience. I've watched The Rich Barber idea and method not only work in my life but also in the lives of barbers who work at The Rich Barber Hair Studio in Sacramento, California.

Being effective and bringing results consistently is inevitable once you make the decision to adopt and apply The Rich Barber Method.

The barbers at the hair studio are individuals who I appreciate and thank for their trust and belief in The Rich Barber idea and principles. They all contributed to The

Rich Barber movement massively. They came and have worked with me at The Rich Barber Hair Studio from the beginning and are walking testimonies to the fact that if you apply the method, and embody The Rich Barber philosophy, you will find success and achieve your potential.

Each of them come from different backgrounds, struggles, ages, and demographics. Adding their own unique talents and abilities. Antoine @dunnthebarber, Isaiah @zaythe_barber, Tyler @tybarbersign, Daniel @dlucs_ Hasheem @hasheemw, plus my two apprentices Joel @jfadeit & Julio @j.marrtt, have all entered this industry and accomplished in a few years what most barbers never do in a lifetime.

Taking The Rich Barber on as an identity will enable you to flourish and grow, but we can't take credit for what you achieve. The method is just words and advice, it is up to you to put in the hard work and make it a reality—just as the barbers listed above have done. I salute those who have gone through the process and found success, and I salute you on your journey to do the same.

When someone is trying to teach me their method for business, productivity, or personal success, I always say, "show me the fruit." Meaning: show me the results, the physical manifestation, and the living embodiment of your claims.

> 'Cut by cut, we distribute self-confidence.'

The results and fruit of The Rich Barber Method exist for everyone to experience. You can touch it, smell it, taste it, see it, and hear it, most of all, **you can BE it**. The time is now, and there has never been a better time—as entrepreneur Gary Vee says— to "crush it and cash in on your passion." You have the opportunity of a lifetime, make sure to execute and implement what you learn quickly and with positive energy.

As for this book, it will be the most valuable tool that you will ever keep at your barber station. Use it daily, as if you could not cut a hair off of a client's head without it.

The Power Of An Idea:
A Letter from Chuka The Barber

Throughout the last six years, I've experimented with an idea about myself. It's an idea that I took on as an identity, and an idea that would shape my beliefs and help guide my actions and decisions.

It's an idea that would pick me up when I would fall, that would challenge me, that would hold me accountable, that would keep me on a path towards success and material gain. This idea forced me to grow and develop, to use my mind and direct me to a fulfilling purpose, and not let me settle for average. It's an idea so grand that it would free me from limitations and replace the poverty mindset which ruled my family for generations.

I wanted an idea that would give me the freedom to control my destiny and my barber career. I sincerely believe that "we become and attract what we think about." So, I took on my idea when I was broke. When nothing about me looked rich—not my car, my clothes, my education or background, not nothing—I began focusing my thoughts on the belief that I am, right this second, the "me" I desire to be in the future.

Then I started a company and called it "The Rich Barber." People that knew me were confused because they didn't see the results of anything "Rich," and people in the barber industry just thought I was some cocky, arrogant barber. They didn't get the concept behind the brand. They didn't know that I was testing The Rich Barber as an idea. They didn't know that I was challenging myself publicly.

It left me no choice but to succeed or perish forever as the barber who called himself Rich but died Broke.

You see, it's not just about money or material gain, it's about self-discovery, new ways of thinking, and using these new ways to navigate the space of barbering for superior results.

If you're someone who's been following my journey since 2012, you've seen the change in me, my career, and in my life. I became The Rich Barber, built the brand, opened up a barbershop that houses some of the hottest barbers in the industry, and invented three innovative products— including my latest game-changing product, the 1-Minute Blade Modifier. I knew it was time to spread the wealth and help thousands of barbers navigate and grow in the barber industry.

What you currently have in your hand is ten years of my experience; trial and error from life, barbering, and entrepreneurship, all combined into a simple, step-by-step method that any barber can use to grow their barber career to heights they never knew were possible.

You have in your hand the tools, the mindsets, the affirmations, and the action steps to attract clients, keep them, and charge more.

Follow it, and don't leave out any steps. Keep this book with you as you build your career, and come back to it often to finetune yourself in all areas of your business.

But first, you must adopt the idea, and claim "I am The Rich Barber." This will be your psychic compass to lead you up the mountaintop of success. Those who succeed are those who believe they can. That belief, paired with your willingness to make the change and pay the price, will make you The Rich Barber.

But you must create it. Belief will not create itself. Claim your new identity, walk it, talk it, manifest it. Think as if you are The Rich Barber.

Follow the method and use the tools. Writer Ralph Waldo Emerson said to "Do the thing, and you shall have the power: but they who do not the thing have not the power."

Once you complete this book, you will have the foundation to earn the right to success. Notice I said *earn*. You must pay the price. Those who take action will have the power. Those who do not, will not. The choice is yours. I know that you can. Now, the only question is: Will you?

What if a simple, straightforward idea could lift you out of your current position and up to a level where you have control over your career and destiny? What if this simple idea could spark new life and action in you, opening up a world of opportunity?

Would you take on this idea? I did. And it worked. There will be thousands of Rich Barbers worldwide. The big question is: Will you be one of them?

Chuka Torres

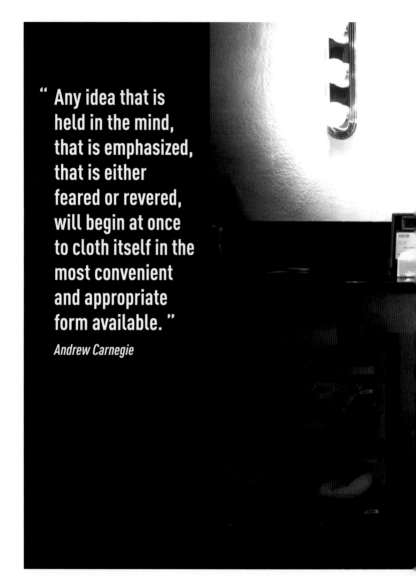

" Any idea that is held in the mind, that is emphasized, that is either feared or revered, will begin at once to cloth itself in the most convenient and appropriate form available. "

Andrew Carnegie

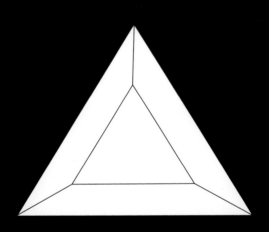

THE RICH BARBER MENTALITY:

HOW THE METHOD WORKS & WHY

The Rich Barber®

When I started The Rich Barber, I was broke, but I had a clear vision in my mind of what I wanted to achieve. Something clicked in me and I realized that success is as much a state of mind as it is the result of hard work and dedication. I realized that I was approaching it the wrong way, and if I wanted to reach my goals, I needed to change my mindset. The first step to you becoming The Rich Barber is taking on that belief, and identity. Then you want to train your mind to live, breathe, and sleep success until The Rich Barber mentality becomes one with you.

My mentality since starting out hasn't changed much, but there's one major difference: Today, I think in a more organized and constructive way. This allows every bit of energy I put out to create a much bigger return than it would have in the early days. Back when I was just starting out, my mindset was hustle hard with ambition. The problem was that is I didn't know how to direct my hustle and ambition to bring about bigger and bigger results. I hustled hard and I was persistent. But I wasn't changing as a person yet, because I still had an old self-defeating mindset about myself and the world that I was holding on to.

Hustle and ambition have always been two driving forces in me that always and only show up under certain conditions. They show up when I have the opportunity to convert my passion into a foundation for financial

success. But even though I grew up in poverty, I've never been the kind of person you could pay to perform any kind of labor that I didn't like to do. If I'm not passionate about the job and the work, and don't see a chance for financial success, I have almost no motivation at all to pursue it. Because of my upbringing, I know how much life sucks when you can't afford what you need. So for me, passion and money have always been synonymous. Passion being the first half of the whole, money being the second half once the passion has been discovered and cultivated.

I wasn't always conscious of this dynamic, but it's been my natural mentality since the start. Once I became fully conscious of this instinct, it became easier to take on other mindsets which would benefit my work, my customers, and therefore my business and my future. Anyone can sporadically put energy and effort into their

> 'When you are driven, focused, and dedicated, everyone can see it the second you walk into the room.'

barber career to reach some kind of success, but to go beyond that, and to do it consciously with a plan, that is when you will begin to develop the real power of The Rich Barber. This is what I did that changed my life and career forever.

But don't play yourself and think that you can cheat. You need to recognize that you will attract the clients, partners, and opportunities which respect and value your skills. When you are driven, focused, and dedicated, everyone can see it the second you walk into the room. But before you can make other people believe in you, you must first believe in yourself. This means you've got to learn how to overcome criticism, constantly reaffirm your own potential, and set clear goals every single day for how to achieve the state of mind known as The Rich Barber mentality.

The Rich Barber mentality is a state of mind you can start to cultivate even before booking your first haircut. A great way to achieve the mentality quickly is to condition your mind with affirmations. Every one of the three domains we cover—The Act of Barbering, Client Experience, and Marketing— has an affirmation which will get you in the right mindset to conquer that domain.

These affirmations will ensure that you consistently enter each domain with a growth mindset, and they will help snap you out of your instinctual behavior and help cultivate the conscious one you need to achieve your goals.

These affirmations—which you can find on page 43, 87, and 119—are some of the most important things you can do to attain the right mindset and lasting habits that will serve you.

In the following chapter, I'll show you how to learn and practice The Rich Barber mentality, and how to use this book to develop your career as a barber. Once you have a grasp on the mentality, you're already halfway there.

> 'The Rich Barber mentality is a state of mind you can start to cultivate even before booking your first haircut.'

" Hard labor and good intentions are not sufficient to carry a man to success, for how may a man be sure that he has attained success unless he has established in his mind some definite object that he wishes."

Napoleon Hill

Why do you need The Rich Barber Method?

Without a clear and specific goal, it is impossible to know if you have become The Rich Barber. And this goes for any goal in life. If you do not define success, you cannot be successful. You need to organize your schedule, your mind, and your skills to bring about the same high-quality results consistently. You need to make sure value is delivered, take stress off of yourself, keep business coming in, and know when to scale prices. The Rich Barber Method is a roadmap for your development as a barber and will provide you with priceless guidance on your journey to control your business, your cuts, and your life.

The Rich Barber Method is designed so that if you follow it exactly you will not fail—it's foolproof. If you use the method, your success will be inevitable.

What is The Rich Barber Method?

In my experience, the majority of barbers don't have a method with which they approach their career. They just get a chair and clippers and start taking appointments and cuttin' hair. This is a surefire way to become *just* a barber, and if becoming a *just* barber is all you want to do, you can put this book down.

> 'One thing to remember is that champions don't happen by accident. Greatness is achieved intentionally, and by design.'

This book is about taking you to that next level, from *just* a barber to The Rich Barber.

Nothing is wrong with being *just* a barber. We are in the service industry, so it's understandable that someone just starting out would make their goal: "Service as many people as possible in order to get paid."

The problem with this kind of thinking is that it's not really thinking at all. It's instinct and imitation. My method will teach you to understand what makes you more or less valuable as a barber, and how to achieve your potential with clear-cut goals.

The Rich Barber is always getting better, and always getting richer. The tools, instructions, and insight in my method will be a source of inspiration and motivation for your entire career. There is always more to learn, and more money to be made. The Rich Barber Method outlines how you can build a successful career that allows you to make as much money as you want, all while living the life you desire.

The Three Domains: How to Create Value as a Barber

The first step to achieving the pinnacle of being The Rich Barber—raising your price—you must focus solely on creating value. As a barber, you create value by developing your skills, engineering a beautiful client experience, and by getting your name out there. The following value-adds constitute the three integral domains you must conquer—and do simultaneously—to become The Rich Barber: The Act of Barbering, Client Experience, and Marketing. By understanding your abilities, your business, and your clients' wants and needs, you create a structure for your service so that it's always a win-win situation.

When I first became a licensed barber ten years ago, the adult price I was charging was $20 per cut. When I had an overflow of clientele, I upped my price up to $30 per cut. Then, when I started to use social media to share and promote my work, it caused an even bigger demand so then I upped my price from $30 to $40. It was then I realized that I could continued to increase my prices and make more money as long as my demand continued to increase for my service. These days I charge $100 plus for a haircut.

One thing to remember is that champions don't happen by accident; greatness is achieved intentionally, and by design. There needs to be a clear plan and obsessive dedication. One thing all of the greats got was paid, and paid a lot more than the rest. Throughout this book, you'll learn what steps you can take to become a great barber and increase your value so that you can up your prices with the confidence that you've mastered your trade in every way possible. You'll be so good that your clients will be excited to pay more for your services.

How Do You Increase Value as a Barber?

Your value increases by understanding the forces that influence your environment. In any industry, raw talent will only get you so far. However, knowing what governs the talent will get you further.

The domains are the spaces in which a barber operates their business. The Act of Barbering, Client Experience, and Marketing are the forces that govern your ability to attract clients, keep them, and charge more.

There is no easy way around mastering The Act of Barbering: You need to learn to use the tools, and you need to be able to duplicate a haircut just by looking at it. There's no easy way around giving your client a

> 'You need to be organized
> and persistent, and before
> you know it, clients will pay
> whatever price you choose
> because your skills, your
> dedication, and your value
> are unquestionably worth it.'

great experience while you're giving them a dope-ass haircut. And walk-in's alone will never allow you to have consistent clientele, so you have to promote yourself and get your name out there. There's no way around any of these responsibilities if you want to be The Rich Barber. But by becoming aware of how things work you can increase your value and track it.

When you understand your profession, what it is a composite of, and you're clear on the desired outcome, then all that's left to do is put your mind to it and do it.

Contrary to popular belief, your value is not increased when you increase the time you spend with clients or give free services. These actions tell the client that you need to go to great lengths in order to justify your prices, rather than by simply offering true value.

Value as a barber comes with striving every day to achieve mastery, and it is definitely needed to reach your goals as The Rich Barber. You need to be organized and persistent, and before you know it, clients will pay whatever price you choose because your skills, your dedication, and your value are unquestionably worth it.

Why Can Some Barber Charge More and Others Can't?

The difference between barbers that can charge more and barbers that can't is the difference between barbers that have conquered the three domains and those that haven't. You must have a firm grasp on your business, you must understand your supply and demand, your clients' needs, and you must understand your level of mastery. Only then can you reasonably decide the maximum price you can charge at any stage in your career.

Some barbers can charge more because they are champions in their field: they must have mastered The Act of Barbering. Some barbers can charge more because their customers have a flawless experience in the chair: they must have engineered a beautiful client experience. And some barbers can charge more because their demand is higher: they must have good marketing. The Rich Barber has checked every one of these boxes and created a foundation for upping their price and reaching their potential. Imagine what would be possible if you conquered all three.

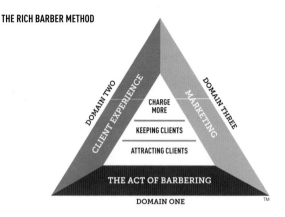

The Developmental Pyramid: How Using the Three Domains Helps Deliver Value

What separates The Rich Barber from a plain ol' barber? That's easy, it's that The Rich Barber is able to raise their prices confidently and consistently until they have achieved the lifestyle they set out for. After you have conquered the three domains and have proved yourself with a world- class client experience, expert marketing techniques, and mastery of The Act of Barbering, then you will begin to move up the center of the pyramid to the final frontier of charging more. The final stages have deceivingly simple steps: Attract Clients, Keep Clients, Charge More.

The better you master the three domains, the faster and easier it will be for you to move up The Developmental Pyramid because you will have proven your value as a barber. The three domains which border the pyramid are the key elements that must be completed in combination in order for the barber to move up the center of the developmental pyramid. The real success and benefits come when the three domains are consciously and consistently applied simultaneously.

Do not neglect a domain because of fear or unfamiliarity. This is common and will vanish with practice. If you want to ensure positive results and maximize your growth as a barber, you must develop and master all three domains. The degree to which you are able to do this will determine how slowly or quickly you climb the center developmental model. Once you're climbing the center of the model—with strong demand for your services and a consistent flow of clientele—you will be able to use the Up Your Price Analysis (Page 150) and charge more with confidence.

Each domain has its own set of rules and habits for positive results. I will also teach you how to use these rules and habits to improve your mindset, layout straightforward action steps, conquer each of the three domains. In each domain, you will find a model to help you conquer that domain. Think of these models as roadmaps to follow on your journey.

Once you have moved up the Developmental Pyramid to the apex of Charging More, you will have developed a strong set of extremely valuable mindsets and habits that will not only allow you to make more money but continue to propel you to higher and higher levels of success in your barber career and in life. All you have to do now is choose where you want to be in your career, decide how much money you want to make, and how much you want to charge per haircut. Visualize what your ideal situation would look like and then follow The Rich Barber Method straight to you coveted goal!

Action Steps:

Money-Making Calculator:

Every great endeavor starts with a goal of some kind. The money-making calculator is a tool to help you set your goals as a barber. Before we get into conquering the three domains, you need to set a monetary goal to aspire to so you understand what exactly you're working towards.

Visit **TheRichBarberMethod.com** and fill out the money-making calculator form. We will help you calculate the prices you need to charge and the number of clients you need to service to meet your income goals.

Next, set a date that you think it's reasonable to hit these goals—maybe a year—and then revisit your numbers and your progress several times a week so you can make sure you are on track and you understand where you are in your growth.

A good way to stay zeroed in on your goals is to enter your money-making calculator results into The Rich Barber Method Self-Confidence formula on the following page (also available at TheRich BarberMethod.com). Print out the formula and hang it by your mirror at home. You need to see it every day, read it aloud to yourself. It might seem weird or uncomfortable at first, but if you do it consistently, you will eventually feel the effects on your mind. This is what it takes to keep yourself on track to achieve a life of freedom, financial success, and fulfillment.

THE RICH BARBER
SELF-CONFIDENCE FORMULA

1. I will generate $................in income by........................(date).

By charging $.................. a cut and working............ days a week.

2. I will do this by being an extremely skilled barber. The best in my city! My cuts are always detailed, tools maintained, and attitude positive. Because of this, I know I will have the power to generate $.................. in income.

3. I know that I have the ability to conquer all three domains of The Rich Barber Method and achieve my goals. Therefore, I will stay persistent and move closer to achieving my goals daily by repeating the mindset affirmations and visualizing my desired outcome for ten minutes in the morning and ten minutes at night.

4. I understand that self-confidence is not given to anyone automatically, it is developed. Therefore, I will develop my self-confidence and overcome fear by stepping out of my comfort zone and continuously taking some form of action that moves me closer to my goal.

5. I realize that I am responsible for my own success and I will get out of barbering exactly what I put in. Therefore, I will pay my dues knowing that the rewards must follow and bring returns which I will have rightfully earned.

6. I will sign my name, commit this formula to memory, and repeat it aloud once a day, with faith that I will attain my goal of becoming **The Rich Barber**.

Signature ....

Date .... **Print Name** ....

THE ACT
OF BARBERING

The Rich Barber®

At ten years old, I picked up a pair of clippers and destroyed my hair for picture day. I still have the elementary school photo to prove it. From then on, I grew up cutting my two brothers' and friends' hair, and my own. Because of this early start, I was pretty good by the time I enrolled in barber college. But now I was constantly learning new things and getting better.

Although the barber college I went to was a small blocked off square section in a swap meet flea market—with nothing but a wood board nailed to the wall to use as a barber station—I made the most of it. I cut every chance I had and learned from every source I could find. To test out new techniques I would watch any YouTube videos that were available at the time, and buy DVDs from barbers who had tutorials. I was really just trying to dissect the whole barbering thing. I would challenge myself to see how quick I could do a bald fade while still making sure that I performed well and it a was good cut. I did this because I know that barber college was preparation for the day I would be professional licensed barber and be able to make some money. In barber college, I became the guy other students would gather around to watch and learn from. My ambition to win drove me to complete barber college with confidence that I had skills.

When I got in my first barbershop, I just knew I could cut and that I was going to be the man. But there was this

one barber in the shop, Rick. I had heard about him but had never seen his work. But when I did, it knocked me right off my high-horse. I was like, *wow, WTF! I have to step my game up.* His level of skills kept his schedule booked and he always had overflow of clientele. We would watch as his clients came through non-stop throughout the day. There were several times when none of us had business, but the waiting room was full of clients waiting for him. We would stand at our stations staring at the door hoping for a walk-in, and when a customer appeared it would always be for him. Literally, the walk-in would pass all six of our empty chairs to book with him, and that never made me feel good. It would eat away at my self-esteem, and I would feel like I was not wanted and rejected. To

> 'My haircuts got more exact and I began to see each client as its own individual work.'

the customers, I wasn't even a option to consider. So I immediately began to figure what it was that I had to do to have the demand that Rick had.

I begin to study Rick while he would cut hair, and when he would walk away from his station after completing a perfect cut, I would go look at his tools, and investigate his clippers to figure out what was making his cuts come out so polished and clean.

I noticed there were two things that he did that really made his haircuts stand out. One was that he paid very close attention to the small details in a haircut, which was something that I didn't do because I didn't think it mattered. I didn't think the details would make it look much better, but they do. Second, he invested in his tools and kept them well maintained as if they were a luxury vehicle. He had modified blades on the trimmers that made his lineups come out super sharp and crispy. He never hesitated to invest in his tools and always made sure his blades stayed cutting like new. Working in the shop next to Rick, I realized I hadn't achieved mastery yet, I settled too soon. But the good thing was: I wanted it and I was ready to work for it.

I didn't dismiss that his haircuts were better than mine. I studied him and saw that every hair mattered and applied his principles. My haircuts got more exact and I began to see each client as its own individual work. God is in the details and that's what his work had way more of than mine: details. So I began to take my time, focus on each client, and really get into what would make them look their best instead of treating everyone like a one-size-fits-all category.

Then Instagram came out and now you can see everybody's work from across the country. Now, it happened again. I thought I had mastered something, and suddenly I'm seeing some work that was just unbelievable from around the world, and I was like *wow*. Again, I used this as motivation, I studied these cuts and strived to achieve them. I strived for that level until I reached that level.

I learned again and again that when striving for mastery, it's important for you to seek out superior work. A master knows that there are always new levels to learn.

'I learned again and again that when striving for mastery, it's important for you to seek out superior work.'

The mastery mindset requires you to pursue and always look to get better at your craft. It won't all be easy, you'll have to overcome criticism—from other people and from yourself. When you're in a shop, you have to give yourself permission to get better. I remember criticizing myself, like, *who am I to get better and try to get this good?* But give yourself permission to grow, and build your own confidence. Know that, in this process, you will be trying real things, and making real progress. You can and will make mistakes, but that's just part of the process.

Michael Jordan said, "I can accept failure, everyone fails at something. But I can't accept not trying. I've failed over and over and over again in my life and that is why I succeed." I think that's a vital part of the mastery mindset. Because even as you try new things to achieve more detail, your clients will notice that there's something different, that you're doing different things, which may at first feel a bit awkward. So give yourself permission to learn and grow, and strive for it every day. That's mastery.

THE ACT OF BARBERING AFFIRMATION:

" I know that I can master The Act of Barbering. Therefore, I will think mastery and strive to achieve mastery of my craft daily."

The Mastery Mindset

Mastery is not only being able to give a great cut but the ability to do so consistently. Mastery is a matter of control and superiority. Mastery is owning your craft. Mastery is when systematic cutting, flawless fades, and all-around perfect cuts are nearly second nature to you. In order to hit this level, you've got to first understand that you're not there yet, and then break down the steps and habits needed to reach your potential and become The Rich Barber.

The first step is to cultivate the mindset of mastery so that your brain, your neurons, your heart, your spirit, and your thoughts are all energized and focussed on attaining mastery. In his book *Outliers*, Malcolm Gladwell says that gaining mastery of anything requires at least 10,000 hours of practice, so you need to plan accordingly and get yourself in the mindset to hit that goal. The greats, in any field, studied, studied, and applied, applied, and constantly perfected the details of their craft. That's what you need to do while watching a barber do their thing. Study a technique, apply it, repeat it, repeat it, and never forget the details.

Being a master means you have dominion over every cut. You enter and end your performance with confidence and ease, but this doesn't happen overnight, it happens, as Rick Ross says, "shootin' in the gym." Do you have what it takes?

Why is Mastery so Important?

If you do your job right, your haircut will make your client feel like a star. No one wants to be walking around with a horrible haircut. I once saw P-Diddy's barber double checking his cut before P-Diddy went on stage; he paid attention to every hair. He was literally chasing him around backstage with a brush. You must act as if every single client is about to go out on stage, and face a crowd of thousands of people with eyes just on them, and your mastery will give them confidence that they look fly.

You can have a great personality and a popular Instagram feed, but if you're not dedicated to becoming a master with the clippers, you will struggle as a barber.

'Gaining mastery of anything requires at least 10,000 hours of practice, so you need to plan accordingly and get yourself in the mindset to hit that goal.'

How to Master Your Trade with a Haircut Muse

When I was starting out, I was inspired by the barbers I saw in school and tin he barbershop I worked at. But I also saw barbers on Instagram doing things I'd never seen before. When you find a barber or photo of a cut that far surpasses your own abilities and the abilities of people around you, then you have found a haircut muse. Whether that muse is a person or a collection of pictures, it's important that you know—visually— what goals you're actually trying to achieve. This is how you create your muse:

- Find and print images of the best haircuts from the most skilled barbers you can find. You can find these on Instagram. Save them in an Instagram collection called 'Haircut Muse,' and look at these pictures every day.
- Make them the background of your phone and computer.
- Take notes on what you like about the haircuts and what impresses you.
- Notice the details, how every hair matters, and the precise styling.
- Notice how you can see the barber's passion, intent, care, and respect in their haircut.
- Look at these muses before and after completing similar cuts.

- Hang them up near your bed, your chair, or
  your bathroom so you are constantly reinforcing
  your goals.

Now, stop reading for a moment, put the book down, and
imagine that you're the one who did that cut. How would
you feel? Would you feel proud? Would knowing you can
give such a great cut give you confidence and motivation?
Would it make you feel good to see your client stand up
from the chair feeling like a million bucks? Would it make
you want to promote and share your work with the world?

Remember this feeling, and approach every cut with the
goal of attaining this feeling for you *and* your client. Search
for this feeling while cutting and when the cut is complete,
check in with yourself and ask yourself: Does it look like
my haircut muse? Am I getting any similar feelings? Was I
mentally present throughout the haircut? Did I do my best?

The haircut muse is what you aspire to, and the goal is to
do a little better with each haircut. Always out-perform all
of your previous haircuts. You'll likely not *always* do better,
but with this mentality, you will develop the awareness and
attention needed to improve rapidly. With a haircut muse,
you now have a way to gauge your cuts and track your
progress.

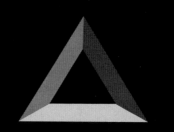

"Success isn't overnight. It's when everyday you get a little better than the day before. It all adds up."

Dwayne "The Rock" Johnson

The Model: The 4 Stages of Achieving Mastery

You can achieve mastery of barbering in four distinct stages which include tools and sanitation; fades, tapers and blends; razors, shaving, and lineups; and enhancements, styles, and designs. Use this model as a guidepost for your progress and to make sure you're checking all the boxes needed to master your craft. Be aware that the first three stages are foundational and extensive, while the fourth is smaller and more of the icing on the cake. That's how I would like you to think about it.

◢ STAGE 1: TOOLS & SANITATION

Mastery means you are set up for success. As barbers, sometimes we overlook our tools. But to gain mastery, you must always keep your tools well maintained. They should be like new and always performing at their best. This is the basics, the stuff you probably learned in barber college. But, just like the three domains lay the foundation for becoming The Rich Barber, becoming an expert in tools and sanitation lays a strong foundation for mastering barbering.

Throughout this chapter, I will outline the tools you'll need at every stage of your development, give you reviews of my favorite products, and cover the industry's most

> ' I choose the clippers and trimmers that I feel are the most versatile so I can keep things very simple.'

popular clippers and trimmers. You should decide which tools best suit you depending on your cutting style and clientele. There are some barbers who keep a clipper and trimmer set of 10+ tools. This could be five trimmers and five clippers that they pick and choose depending on the task at hand or the client's hair type.

As for me, I prefer to work with a set of three, maximum four: a trimmer, an adjustable clipper, and a balding clipper. I choose the clippers and trimmers that I feel are the most versatile so I can keep things very simple. That's just my style and preferred set up. (Note: I'm only speaking about clipper and trimmers here, not other tools like razors and shears). This doesn't mean I don't own more than three or four clippers and trimmers total, it just means I don't have more than three or four tools set up at my station at one time.

Having more or fewer tools is neither good nor bad, it just depends on what you prefer and what increases your efficiency. I am more efficient and effective when I keep things very simple, but some other barbers may be more efficient and effective with more variety. I suggest that you try multiple trimmer and clippers until you discover your dream team of tools. Then, once you know what your go-to

> 'Once you have blended tools and technique into a haircutting method, you will have laid the foundation for achieving mastery in The Act of Barbering.'

tools are, you can eventually merge this right into your Systematic Cutting Method. This is very important because once you have blended tools and technique into a haircutting method, you will have laid the foundation for achieving mastery in The Act of Barbering.

Sanitation:

Keeping your tools clean is vital for a smooth operating business, great haircuts, and state regulatory boards. We won't spend too much time on this since every state has different rules and you probably learned a lot of this in barber college. Make sure to routinely brush up on your state's rules. It's not just legal hoops to jump through, it will help keep your tools fresh, your station clean, and your clients happy.

The most important part of sanitary barbering is disinfecting. You need to always make sure to read the manufacturer's directions for their tools, they often have special insight on how to sanitize particular products. You also need to remember that Quats, phenol, and other disinfectants all have different mixture ratios. Here are seven easy steps for keeping your tools clean using Quats solution, courtesy of Edgar Fernando Borunda Villagran.

1. Mix Quats Solution into the water at a ratio of 1.25 ounces for every gallon of water. Always add the water first and then the disinfectant, to reduce bubbles.
2. Make sure to remove all hair from the brushes, combs, guards, razors, and other tools you will be disinfecting. It's good to use a cleaning brush or compressed air to remove all the hairs.
3. Wash them with hot water and soap, preferably antibacterial soap.
4. Rinse and dry your instruments very well. This stage is called sanitation and it's the first step towards total disinfection.
5. Put your tools into the disinfectant mixture and make sure the tools are completely immersed.
6. Leave the tools for 10–15 minutes before removing and rinsing very well.
7. Dry each tool with a clean towel and also let air dry. Store them in a sealed container until your next use.

These seven steps are the basics of sanitation, but again, it's important to know your state's rules and make sure you're acting in accordance with their regulations. Make sure to disinfect your tools every day after work so you have a fresh set in the morning. Some might even keep a duplicate of every tool in case you'd rather do it less often.

Your clients will notice if your tools are old and dirty. Keeping your tools sanitized is good for your client, good for you, and good for your tools. Take it seriously.

Clippers:

I always get a special feeling when I get a new pair of clippers. As barbers, our tools become a real-life extension of us, so it's very important that you select with the utmost care the clippers that you can rely on and become one with. In this section I'll give you a list of the best and most widely used by myself and the industry's top barbers. You can't go wrong with any of them but choose according to your preference.

Andis Masters:

Chuka's Review: If you want a proven, solid clipper that can take on any cut and style with ease, you can't go wrong with Masters. They are overall great clippers and are housed in a sturdy aluminum body. Just remember that it feels like a machine and acts like one, which means it sometimes acts up and can be difficult to tune up and fix. But when it's well maintained, it's a beast. And when used with the magnetic guards, things get even better because you get smooth and consistent cuts. The high-speed magnetic motor clipper gets a bit hot sometimes but it delivers 14,000 cutting strokes per minute and a single lever adjusts blade from 000 to 1.

Andis Fade Masters

Chuka's Review: This is a great clipper to use along with regular Masters or even by itself. You can achieve some unbelievable blends with the fade blade. The shaping and sculpting ability is unmatched, but I would not recommend this be your only clipper just because it's not versatile enough. It also cuts at 14,000 strokes per minute and has a single lever which adjusts the blade from 00000 to 000. The magnetic guards aren't a perfect fit on the fade blade and it's a bit tougher than most to align, adjust, and set the blades. Still, it's powerful, durable, and great for both tight fades and heavy-duty cutting.

Wahl Cordless Seniors:

Chuka's Review: This is a superior clipper and is one that any barber would enjoy working with. The 5 Star Cordless Senior is a one of a kind clipper with its precision fade blades, metal bottom housing, and cord/ cordless capabilities. Its powerful rotary motor results in higher blade speed for tackling thick hair. The 5 Star Cordless Senior offers a 70-minute run time and it fits nicely in the hand. I find it to be a perfect weight and very versatile for all around cutting and styles.

Wahl Magic Clip Cordless:

Chuka's Review: This is a great clipper for all-around cutting and any style. Very similar to the Cordless Senior, it has a cord/cordless cutting capability and a 90-minute run time. Sometimes it feels a bit delicate for my tastes and I'm not a huge fan of the wedge blade it comes with, but it's lightweight, compatible with Wahl premium guards, and doesn't overheat.

Wahl Balding Clippers:

Chuka's Review: Great for what it's specifically made to do: balding. It's the perfect alternative to using trimmers for balding. If you would like it to be cordless, just put the balding blade onto a Cordless Senior or Magic Clip and then you will have a cordless balding clipper. It cuts surgically-close.

BaBylissPRO® GOLD/ROSE FX Clipper

Chuka's Review: This clipper is super light, cuts crisp, and runs cordless for 2 hours. I think that an adjustment locking lever could be beneficial, but for some barbers, they may see it as restriction of the free flow you get with Andis Master and Wahl senior levers. GOLDFX is a cord/cordless lithium clipper. The perfect tool for cutting all hair types.

Oster's Fast Feeds

Chuka's Review: This is a great and reliable clipper that performs well in a variety of scenarios. It's got a super quiet motor if that's important to you, but this does result in a good amount of vibration in your hand. It is ultra-durable and built for long-lasting performance. It's got an adjustable blade size from 000 to 1 and you can expect a smooth, clean, and uniform cut.

Trimmers:

You got to make sure your trimmers are "hitters" and they give you the detailed precision you need to complete each job with mastery. These tools are a part of us barbers, and we won't be complete without a reliable pair. Below, I give my reviews on the industry's best and most widely used. Again, you can't go wrong with any of them. Choose what feels right for you.

Andis Slimline Pro Li:

Chuka's Review: The Slimline Pro is overall great trimmer with versatility, great design, and cordless freedom. It's got a rotary motor with 6,000 strokes per minute and a long run time. I wouldn't recommend it for big jobs because it's too small, but it is great for edging longer hair and detailing.

Andis T-outliner Cordless:

Chuka's Review: Although getting the blades set right can be frustrating for some, once it's done, this trimmer is superior when it comes to pure power, speed, and overall performance. The rotary motor runs at 7,200 strokes per minute and it has a 100-minute runtime.

T-retros:

Chuka's Review: This is my personal favorite Wahl trimmer. The Retro T-Cut features an adjustable t-wide blade to produce quicker and more precise cutting results. This lightweight trimmer is an excellent go-to for lineup details and design work. Apart from the fact that there is no charge light to indicate the battery level, it's a really fun trimmer to work with.

Heros:

Chuka's Review: Corded and powerful, the Hero Trimmer cuts hair with speed and ease. It features a t-blade, fits in the palm of your hand for optimal control and comfort, and is perfect for lining, artwork, and creating custom styles.

BaBylissPRO® ROSEFX Trimmer

Chuka's Review: This super powerful cord/cordless trimmer can be a main trimmer but you may want a complimentary trimmer for where this one lacks in sharpness and detail. It is a perfect tool for outlining, designs and all other fine work. It boasts an amazing 3-hour runtime, an all-metal housing with a knurled barbell grip, and it's capable of taking down bulk with ease.

Bevel:

Chuka's Review: This cordless trimmer is beautifully designed and very innovative. An overall great trimmer with a more than 4-hours of runtime and easy blade adjustments.

When to use Detachable Blade Clippers:

These are very powerful and efficient for removing bulk and long hair. They are also good for the clipper-over-comb technique as well as cutting wet or dry hair. It's a bit time consuming to switch the blades out and they aren't very good for detailed fading and tapering because there is no free-range adjustment lever. Sanitation of each blade after use is also time-consuming. It's not a must-have, but they can be beneficial if you see fit for your style. I tried them once but never cared to use them afterward.

'You got to make sure your trimmers are 'hitters' and they give you the detailed precision you need to complete each job with mastery. These tools are a part of us barbers, and we won't be complete without a reliable pair.'

Shavers:

Great for finishing fades and removing stubble.

My favorite three (all quite similar):

- Wahl Finale Finishing Tool
- BaBylissPRO® FOILFX02™
- Andis ProFoil Lithium

Razors:

Not much difference between the razors on the market. You should get a standard razor and an exposed blade razor.

Shears:

Professional hair cutting scissors can be expensive. A pair of shears costing $1,000 is not unheard of in the industry. Depending on your preferred way of cutting, you should decide what kind of shears you need, and what the quality of the shear should be. If you are mostly a clipper barber, then you may not need or want to spend $1000 for each pair of shears. You may only need a midrange quality shear. If you are someone who will use shears almost as much or more than you use clippers, then you should go with the top grade shears. Either way, a barber should have at least one main shear.

When shopping for shears, you should look at the quality of the steel. I've ranked the steel below from top grade to lower-grade: Hitachi ATS 314, Hitachi 440C, V10 (VG10), V1 (VG1), 440C, 440A.

Here is a list of the most widely used types of shears and how they are used:

1. **Main:** This shear is typically 5.5 or 6 inches in length and is the go-to scissor for most of your work.
2. **Thinner:** This shear can vary from 27 to 40 teeth and is used for blending and removing lines.
3. **Texturizer:** Varying from 10 to 24 teeth, a texturizing shear is used for removing weight and creating volume.
4. **Long shear:** This shear is usually 6-7 inches long and is used for specialized cutting techniques such as scissor-over-comb, deep point-cutting, and heavy-duty blunt cutting.
5. **Narrow blades:** This shear is usually 5–5.5 inches long with narrower blades for intricate detail work.
6. **Backup tool:** This tool should be as good as your main cutting tool. A proper backup is a must when you send in your go-to shear in for service.

What's the difference between thinning and texture shears?

Texturizing Shears

These shears typically have 10 to 24 wide and further distanced teeth. The wider teeth cut more hair, making this type of tool perfect for bangs and whisping. The cut section of hair will be visible compared to the uncut section. A texture shear is used to remove the bulk and create more lift and movement. The underlying cut sections of hair will support the uncut hair. The more aggressive texture shears can have anywhere from five to nine teeth. These tools cut a more significant gap into hair sections creating a more obvious texture between the cut and uncut hair.

Thinning Shears

These are the best shears for blending away scissor marks in the hair. The thinner teeth remove less hair with each cut allowing these shears to remove weight without increasing volume. Unlike the texture shear, there will be no visible difference between the cut and uncut sections of hair. Thinning shears are often used to create feathering and a more soft finish.

As with any other shear, it is very important to use thumb-only action when using these specialized tools. Squeezing the blades together can cause a tooth to catch on the cutting blade, making it impossible to close the

> 'When shopping for shears, you should look at the quality of the steel.'

shear and damaging both blades, taking years off the life of your tool.

Finally, you should take very good care of your shears by following this maintenance procedure:

- Wipe them after every use and clean them at the end of each day. Chemicals can dull your blades, while hair and dirt left on your shears can cause rusting and pitting.
- Oil shears daily in the screw area.
- Check tension daily and adjust as needed. (If the shear bends hair it usually means that the shear is too loose. New shears will need adjustment after the first few cuts as the screws and washers set in place.)
- Keep the blades closed when not in use or when setting the shear down. An open shear exposes the fragile edges to nicks or bends.
- Only cut hair! Any other material can bend or nick the edges.
- Store shears in a case.
- Check edges for nicks by gently running the tip of your fingernail along the blades.

STAGE 2: FLAWLESS FADES, TAPERS, AND BLENDS

Almost every haircut is going to involve a fade, taper, or blend, so it's super important you get them down perfectly. Below are five essential steps you've got to conquer to move beyond this stage.

- **Remove Enough Hair**
  When you're just starting out, I know it's frightening because once it's gone, there's no going back. But that's part of the job. If you want it to be nice and tight, you need to do it. Don't be afraid if its not perfect the first couple times, you'll get it right and it will make your life easier and your cuts better.

- **Blend Tight**
  Blending tight goes hand and hand with removing enough hair. This way, the hair is at a controlled length that holds its contrast. In order to do this, blends must be tight at the lower section of the fades, tapers, and blends.

- **Stay in Control and Be Consistent Throughout the Blend**
  Keep the blend/taper/fade uniform to the initial guideline. You do this by taking your time and applying systematic cutting which will keep you

> 'Almost every haircut is going to involve a fade, taper, or blend. So, it's super important you get them down perfectly.'

from jumping around with the clipper stokes. Find out more about systematic cutting on page 77.

- **Know Your Clipper & Go With Its Tempo**
  To get the cleanest cuts, you must become one with your tools. What I mean by this is that don't go too fast or too slow with the strokes of the clipper, find the optimal tempo of each stroke to allow the clipper to cut at its full potential. Then, in time, you will be able to feel your way through in knowing the right tempo by the way that the clipper and the client's hair reacts to one another. Then, you and your clipper are one. When you able to do this, you will notice how much cleaner your haircuts will be.

- **Take Pictures and Compare**
  Haircut muses (more on page 46) are important for perfecting your blends. Always take pictures of your haircuts and compare them to your favorite barbers' haircut blends so you know if you're on target or not.

"I will not lose, for even in defeat, there's a valuable lesson learned, so it evens up for me."

Jay-Z

STAGE 3: RAZOR, SHAVING & LINEUPS

Razor Work & Shaving

Razor work should be developed and mastered because it will be a vital fundamental skill to your craft. As to what services you decide to offer that involve a razor is up to you. You can do the full-service shave with the steam, hot towel, and lather, or just use the razor for the details of a haircut or line up. Or even do both. It's totally up to you. There are two main types of razors that barbers use: the single-edge razor holder which holds a single-edge blade and the safety razor holder which is a t-shape razor that can hold a single or a double-edge blade.

Lineups and Outlining

The lineup—or the outline—is the process of shaping the edges of the hair around the haircut or beard area to give a cleaner detailed look to the haircut or beard. It's important for the lineups to have symmetry and, in many cases, sharpness. Two things make lineups difficult. One, heads are not flat surfaces, and two, all head shapes and hairlines are different. So, to master them. you must learn how to approach a lineup to achieve a completely uniform look to the overall haircut. A bad lineup can ruin a good haircut just as a bad haircut can ruin a good lineup. You must learn how to approach the lineup and how to best use your trimmer to maneuver the outline process for precise

cutting. This takes time and practice. Always know how you plan to approach the line up before you do. You can do this by taking the time first to examine the hair and decide on the steps you need to take before starting the lineup process.

STAGE 4: PLAYING WITH ▰ ENHANCEMENTS, STYLES, DESIGNS

I want to cover enhancements first in this stage because this addition to your skill set should come as soon as possible. Enhancements should improve your already good work, not to be used to cover up bad work. It's very important that your client is still fresh after the temporary enhancement is gone. If it was used as a substitute for real skill, it will do more harm to your business than it will do good. This is why temporary enhancements is not in Stage 2. Make sure you're really good at Steps 1–2 before playing too much with enhancements.

When I played basketball, I learned how to dribble and score before I was doing slam dunks. You must know the fundamentals of the game before making it fancy. Think of enhancements in the same way. The goal is to score with a great haircut first, then once you're able to do that, you can finesse it and take it to the next level.

I'm not saying this to scare you away from the attempt or fear trying, all I'm saying is that if you give strong attention and focus on the fundamentals you will eventually have the foundation that all champions are built from. On the following pages, I'll outline some of the most popular enhancements.

Temporary Enhancements

Hair Fibers

This should be the first enhancement you try. It is the most widely used temporary enhancement that comes in a powder-like form. It's used to give a fuller look by filling in thin hair and light spots, and also a general enhancement to the haircut. Hair fibers can be applied with a spray applicator or sprinkle top. Most barbers use the applicator. Fibers are then held in place with a holding spray.

Hair fibers are perfect for amateur to advanced barbers. When used properly, they give a very natural look and can take any haircut to the next level. If you are new to enhancements, hair fibers are perfect for practice, because the fibers are easily removed with a brush or comb if it's prior to applying the hold spray. You can treat the fibers just like hair when lining up.

You will have a lot of fun with hair fibers and your clients will love you for it. One of the best things about hair fibers is that you can apply them quickly. You can include hair fibers as a complimentary part of your service or charge extra for it. It's complimentary with my service not just because it washes out, but because I want them to have it. Remember, it's quick to do, makes your work stand out, and your clients will love it. So it's a win-win situation.

Semi-Permanent Hair Dye

This is a liquid dye that can last three or four days even with light washing. Usually, it's applied with either an air compressor or a color application brush. It's often left in by the barber and the client washes it out at home. Just like hair fibers, it can be used on thinning hair, light spots, or simply as a haircut enhancement or style. This is a liquid so it is can be a bit tough to work with at first, but once you get it down you're good to go. This is a service that I would charge for. It takes more time and effort but it lasts multiple days. You can really take your cut to the next level and have your client coming back for more.

Permanent Color and Enhancements

Permanent Hair Dye

This permanent color dye is either in liquid form or powder which is mixed into a liquid. This dye can be used as a style enhancement but also for covering up white/grey hairs. The permanent dye is usually washed out by the barber, especially if it's being used to cover white hairs. Other than washing it, and the time needed to allow the color to set in permanently, permanent color can be very similar to the semi-permanent in terms of the process. There are other ways of doing color but that goes beyond what we are covering in this section and book. When it comes to enhancements and color, this service will take the most time and effort and should come with an additional cost.

Designs

Designs are in Stage 3 because they have the ability to enhance a cut the same way color does. Designs are a great way to give individuality and expression to a haircut.

A design could be as simple as a unique part or as complex as a logo or face portrait. But for the majority of barbers, this will be more of a simple part to a light abstract design. Designs can also include fading and tapering to give it more life and contrast. Light designs can be played within Stage 2, but you should really wait until you have mastered your lineups. If you can't do a basic lineup or don't have great control of the trimmer, then odds are you will ruin a design.

Advanced Styling & Styles

What I mean by advanced styling and styles is the creative aspect of the finish. It could be something like texture, structure, slanted Gumby-style high-top fade, creative design, and so on.

That's what I mean by this. You always want to give the client a complete finished look, but once you got that down and mastered, at this next stage you may want to show off a bit and finish off with a slam dunk.

Creating Your Own Styles

This is where all your hard work and dedication come together. At this stage, you get to really show your art and build a name for yourself. This is where you will begin to contribute to the forward development of the industry. I believe this is where barbers can become industry leaders through their craft. This is when you're able to get on YouTube or Instagram and call a masterpiece you created "The God Fade," and then watch as other barbers imitate it on their clients and tag you. This is what barbering is about, but this won't happen overnight. Build yourself and your skills until you can help take our industry to the next level by creating your own styles that inspire others.

'This is what barbering is about,
but this won't happen overnight'

Action Steps:

- **Schedule Out Study Days & Times
  to Hit Your Goals**
  You should be able to look back at each
  week's schedule and see exactly how many
  hours you dedicated to improving your craft.

- **Subscribe to The Rich Barber Mixtape**
  You'll find step-by-step tutorials from
  the hottest barbers executing their best
  techniques that will help you improve yours
  absolutely free! To gain access instantly, go
  to website **TheRichBarberMethod.com.**

  Also subscribe and click the bell on our
  YouTube channels:
  https://www.youtube.com/user/chukt916.
  This way you will have access to all of the
  previous mixtape tutorials and
  stay connected.

- **Create Your Systematic Steps & Practice!**
  Being systematic is vital. It gives you a
  reliable process to approach each haircut.
  It will make you more thorough and confident.
  It is integral to developing mastery because it's
  a set of broken down steps that you repeat and
  are able to master.

  My systematic steps are as follows:

  - Prep The Hair
  - Trim
  - Guidelines
  - Blends
  - Line Up Razor
  - Enhancements
  -Touch Up

  Would yours be any different? If so,
  write them out so every cut is predictable,
  repeatable, organized, and results in
  the best cut and the best client experience.

- **Print out your affirmation and repeat it daily.**

DOMAIN TWO

CLIENT EXPERIENCE

You are selling a feeling! You are creating an experience that ultimately leads to an emotional feeling that the client is left with. Yes, they come for the haircut but they keep coming for the feeling. You want your service to create a feeling that they can only get coming to you.

It's hard to create this feeling if you haven't felt it as a client. I believe it's important to go to places that treat you like royalty so you gain that awareness of what a great client experience feels like.

Often barbers don't understand that they are destroying their business because they don't understand what influences its growth. They need to take responsibility for their business's structure and they must have a plan. A vital part of a successful barber business is to have full understanding and control of their clients' experiences.

We're in the people business, and that means you have to build relationships and there is no way around it. You have to care, that's why the affirmations and the self-confidence formula are so vital. They allow you to build yourself up so can be the kind of barber that creates a world-class client experience.

When they come in after a bad day, you turn that around and don't allow their bad mood to affect yours. Actually, you try and be the thing to improve their mood. You control the situation; always go into it realizing that

> '**I realized that if I wanted to be unique and bring more value to my customers, I had to work on my personality and make sure it connects with my goals.**'

they come to you for rejuvenation and self-confidence. I realized that if I wanted to be unique and bring more value to my customers, I had to work on my personality and make sure it connects with my goals. I took pride in leaving my customers feeling confident and re-energized, with an increased belief in themselves, as if they could make happen whatever they wanted in their lives.

This attitude I took on added a layer to my business because it affected my character. I was more aware, positive, and conscious of the energy I put out. This allowed me to exhibit the vibe I wanted people to feel in my chair.

In my ten years, I've seen barbers limit their grown and earning potential because they lacked vital parts of the client experience.

The following are stories of real-life barbers that I have witnessed unknowingly destroying their business's opportunities for growth.

Your Appearance Matters

When he came in for work, Larry never really cared about his appearance. He wore shabby clothes that were baggy and worn out. It never made sense to me. We're in the business of making people look good, yet he never cared to look good himself. Your potential customers need to be impressed with how fresh you look. They need to see that increase manifested in their barber. You want to project confidence and high self-esteem.

Your potential clients need to look at you and think that you have something they want, and that you are the one to give it to them: a fresh cut and a priceless feeling about themselves.

What I noticed about Larry was that his clients cared as much about their appearance as much as he did: They were not really concerned, therefore, they were not willing to pay much because they didn't value their appearance, or the experience. Because of this, he is unable to charge more, his clientele remains inconsistent and he relies mostly on walk-ins.

I'm not saying you need to be a suit and tie barber, but The Rich Barber must strive to look like someone their ideal client wants to be or respects. Clients need to look up to your appearance so they will trust you to give them the same quality look.

Your Personality Matters

Bran was a decent barber, but his business struggled because he had a lifeless personality and didn't work to improve his relationship with clients and customers. He addressed them with a low-energy, monotone voice. Because his behavior wasn't very welcoming, he would snag a random walk-in, but he would rarely keep them as recurring clients.

He didn't work to bring life or enthusiasm to his client experience at all.

When he would take walk-ins, he wouldn't even introduce himself and he would just say, "Yeah, um, I got you," but showed no interest in the client as a person.

His haircuts were usually decent, but it wasn't an experience that made people want to return to him. His approach was so careless, and he acted like he didn't need their business.

He would be in the shop from early until late—seven days a week—but then acted as if his clients were peasants. Watching the way he interacted with clients made me feel uncomfortable because it was so awkward. I can't remember hearing him have a conversation, and I watched him struggle because he couldn't create a connection.

'The Rich Barber must care about building a relationship with customers, so he or she is in a perpetual state of attracting and retaining clients.'

He never won people over because he didn't care, and he wasn't excited to see them, so they weren't excited to see him.

The Rich Barber must care about building a relationship with customers, so he or she is in a perpetual state of attracting and retaining clients.

Your System Matters

Finally, Derek was another barber with a sustainable clientele and pretty good demand, but he was not at all a smooth operator. He had a pleasing personality, but his booking and appointment system was a mess, and this brought him stress, which made getting cuts by him also stressful. There was no structure to his business flow.

He would always be running behind schedule. I'm talking an hour or hour-and-a-half late for appointments. Because of this, his clients would often be just as inconsistent as him because he was training them in bad behavior, and his system wasn't building trust with them. If you're always late, your clients will always be late, and your schedule will be a mess.

He was never clear about the structure of his appointments and communication. He would approve a text or call appointment without checking who booked him online, and then two people would come at the same time. He would say, "I'll get you in," and he would work late hours to make sure all his clients were served, but it wouldn't be at the time they booked. This is not a sustainable business.

This disorganization caused stress for both him and his customer, and always backtracking on his word made him unable to scale his business and charge more. He never paid attention to the operations, and he allowed the dysfunction to become normal. Unorganized and scattered structure creates unorganized and scattered clients.

'If you're always late, your clients will always be late, and your schedule will be a mess.'

> 'You've got to take your client experience seriously; a good cut or sweet Instagram feed is not enough to build a sustainable business.'

The Rich Barber must be clear about their schedule, business flow, and expectations so that their appointments are reliable, consistent, and organized.

These stories should be warnings for new and established barbers. You've got to take your client experience seriously; a good cut or sweet Instagram feed is not enough to build a sustainable business. Your personality, your appearance, and your business flow all need to be on point to increase your value as a barber. If you value yourself as a person, and a barber, you will be overall more attractive to your clients because they will see that you value yourself and take your work and their experience seriously.

You need to remember that you're in the service industry and at the end of the day, even if you haven't reached mastery in your haircuts, a smooth client experience will ensure clients still have a great time in your chair from start to finish.

THE CLIENT
EXPERIENCE
AFFIRMATION:

" I will deliver world-class service and treat my clients like royalty."

The World Class Service Mindset

World-class service is not an accident; it is by design. Anyone who knows how to be of amazing service to others does it intentionally. They know what their customers want and need before they even have time to ask. World-class service providers understand their industry and customers through and through.

At a world-class hotel, the guest turns around and "bam" a hand is out to take their bags. At a world-class restaurant, it's the waiter that is so attentive to your glass that it never runs dry while enjoying bottomless mimosas at Sunday brunch. The party goes on with no interruptions and you have no idea how many glasses you've had. You end up taking an Uber home and passing the fuck out. Haha! Then you wake up with a story to tell.

Most of all, world-class service requires genuine care. The more you care about the value (service) you provide, how that value is delivered, and how it's communicated to the customer, the better your overall service experience will be. So, make sure to care about your client in every aspect of your business.

The moment a customer begins to interact with any part of your business, the experience begins; whether that's a photo of you, a haircut you did, or the landing page on your booking website.

Clients start to create their own perception of how they feel about you, your services and business. Each interaction builds a layer to the experience that the client will unconsciously or consciously feel a certain way about. The goal of this section is to teach you how to create an experience throughout. World-class service treats clients like royalty, and it's genuine. It's so well developed in the person's or company's makeup that it flows naturally.

Why does Your Service Have to be World Class?

Apple founder Steve Jobs said it best when he said: "You have to care." World-class service requires that you care more than most. Customers can tell if you are half-stepping with your service. Caring and having certain systems in place will take you from simply getting clients to keeping them.

There it is, plain and simple. In order to approach your service with a world-class mindset: You have to **CARE**. You have to care about what you do; you have to care about your customer and the experience they're having with you. When you genuinely care, it will not go unnoticed, and it's almost impossible for it to go unappreciated.

"You can make more friends in two months by becoming interested in other people than you can in two years by trying to get other people interested in you."

Dale Carnegie

I agree with Steve Jobs that there is something very powerful about the simple act of caring. The effects of caring about the little details have immeasurable results in the experience you create for your clients. Make sure that you take pride in serving others and delivering a one-of-a-kind experience so that you deliver a special feeling that can't be duplicated. This attitude will eventually go beyond service and will benefit all that you do in your barber career.

To develop the world-class service mindset, ask yourself the following questions:

- What is world class service?
- What does it feel like?
- How does it feel differently from a service like Bran, Larry, and Derek's?
- How can I do it?

I've heard barbers ask so many times: "How do I get more customers?" This isn't a bad question, but all too often they are so concerned with how they can "get more customers" that they lose focus on consistently delivering a world-class service to their current clients. It's human nature to stop improving what is familiar and get comfortable. But getting comfortable stagnates your business; high-quality service attracts high-quality clients. Taking good care of your clients and delivering a great experience is a big deal and it makes a big difference to your business.

It Starts With Your Positive Personality Habits

Your personality is so important. If it's attractive, you will attract, if it's not, you will repel. Pay attention to your tone of voice and body language.

Below is a list of positive personality habits that will help you build an attractive personality, positively influence your clients, and add to your overall client experience. Do these consistently until they are woven into your character and you exhibit them habitually.

There will also be friction in your business at times, but it's important you always maintain your world-class service. So, I have also included a special list of positive personality habits specifically for helping you deal with client friction. Print these, learn these, and study them until they are natural.

> 'Caring and having certain systems in place will take you from simply getting clients to keeping them.'

Positive Personality Habits

- Acknowledge the client as they enter the shop.
- Greet your client by name and with a smile.
- Understand the Golden Rule: Treat others as you would have them treat you.
- Give genuine compliments and give them generously. (This does not mean engage in fake flattery, instead, become genuinely interested in every client.)
- Be an attentive listener and encourage them to talk about themselves. Ask questions they will enjoy answering and give exclusive attention because nothing is more flattering than that.
- Always treat clients like royalty. You are at their service, and you need to pay attention to the small things to treat them lavishly.
- Ask for updates about things they mentioned last time (work, family, and so on).
- Discover their interests and accomplishments and talk about them.

'Be an attentive listener and encourage them to talk about themselves.'

Positive Personality Habits for Dealing with Friction

- Always give them the benefit of the doubt
- Have a place that clearly outlines policies and procedures. If a client misses an appointment or is a no-call no-show, let them know you have a system, and procedures, for making and canceling appointments, and how easy it is for them to do in the future.
- Show the client how the policies benefit them if they have an issue.
- Admit when you're wrong or have made a mistake. They will appreciate your acknowledgment of the situation and forgive you.
- Bring suggested solutions but never attack the client with criticism or emphasize their mistake or problem.

'Bring suggested solutions but never attack the client.'

The Model: How to Stage the Experience to Create 'The Feeling'

You can create the feeling of royalty and world-class service in four distinct stages.

STAGE 1: YOUR APPEARANCE & YOUR PERSONALITY

Appearance is part of your personality, so you need to do whatever you can to look good. Your clothes are a part of your personality. As Mark Twain said, the "clothes make the man. Naked people have little or no influence on society." You don't have to be a shirt and bowtie barber (I'm not), but you should look clean, like you can cut some MF'n hair.

People go to the barber to look after their appearance, why would they go to you if you don't look after yours? Dress nice and clean, and you will stand out.

Your personality should also attract, so make sure you're reading the personality habits. You gotta have a pleasing personality, and people need to feel good in your chair. In order to get this, you need to identify how clients react to the way you do and say things.

Their feedback—negative and positive—will allow you to have more harmony in your relationships.

STAGE 2: WINNING ENVIRONMENT

A winning environment is foundational. You need to make sure your barbershop is one that promotes positivity and growth. At The Rich Barber Hair Studio, we keep the good vibes poppin! When you come get a haircut there, you get excited about life and your ideas. We're here to uplift. A winning environment is one that is already set up for success. It's organized, it's automated, and it always allows you to run a smooth operation.

You need to make sure that you work in a winning environment that makes you and your client's souls feel fed throughout every interaction.

Finding Your Perfect Barbershop:

All shops aren't created equal. Make sure you establish yourself at a shop where you can grow and demand higher prices throughout your growth. If you are a great barber, and the others in the shop are subpar, it would be whack if you had to charge the same as them. As Gary Vee would say: "Your shit is broke." And you'll be broke too. I believe if your work is better and you hustle harder, then you deserve to reap the benefits. Do what you have to do to make sure your situation is right.

Start by asking yourself: What would my dream barbershop look like? What kind of environment would it have? Does it fit my personality? How does it make you feel? What kind of conversations would you have? What kind of client does your perfect shop attract?

Write the answers down! And keep a clear image of that barbershop in your mind as you search for the right barbershop.

When you go to check out some barbershops in your city and see if there are spaces available, not only should you spend some real time inside the walls of the shop, but offer to take the shop owner to coffee or something. The owner really sets the standard for the shop, taking them out will let you know if you two connect.

Harmony is key in a place you're going to spend five to seven days out the week at. Be aware of the atmosphere you're trying to be a part of.

Ask yourself questions like:
- Is this a place that will influence me to thrive?
- Is this an environment where I will enjoy my craft?
- How was I welcomed as a potential new barber or stylist?
- What's the conversation like?
- How do I feel about the clientele?
- Do they serve my ideal clientele?
- How do the workers interact which each other?
- Is it commission or booth rent?

> 'Harmony is key in a place you're going to spend five to seven days out the week at.'

Spend some time with the barbers as well. Ask them questions about what the culture is like, what the walk-in system is, and other questions to get a good feel for what it's like to work there.

Then rate each barbershop you visit on a scale from 1 to 10 and see who ranks the best!

Remember, this is all preference, ultimately it ends up being what is **right for YOU**. There isn't a right or wrong for the barbershop you choose, just make sure it's somewhere you will thrive.

Your Barber Station:

Make sure your station is organized and that you have everything at your fingertips. Refer to page 54 for ideas or advice for trimmers, clippers, and shavers. As for the rest of your barber station, just make sure you have what you need when you need it. It is so important that you're not borrowing someone else's Cool Care or razors when you're performing a haircut. Having a cleanly organized barber station allows you to give your full attention to the haircut and your world-class service.

" At The Rich Barber Hair Studio we have no set prices that all barbers must charge. Each barber is allowed to charge what they feel they are worth based on the demand they create for their services."

Chuka The Barber

STAGE 3: SYSTEM

Run your business don't let it run you. A consistent business model and a good system will train your customers. You may need to serve everyone at the beginning, but eventually, you want to be serving only your ideal clients. An ideal client is a person who understands, respects, and admires your business model.

This is why creating a system is so important: it can help turn any client into your ideal client.

Have Automated Communication

Whenever the customer comes in contact with you, their experience should be clear, pleasant, and leave them with zero questions. The customer should know exactly where to book, where you're located, how much you charge, and what kind of services you offer. The customer should be very clear on how you run your business; this is the first step to training your client, building ideal clientele, and staying in control of your business.

Your automated communication is the first filter for clients. You need to set up your rules and stick to them.

Here's a list of everything that should be automated (preferably in a booking app):

- Location
- Schedule and availability
- Prices, as well as any additional fees for other services
- Payment processing
- Late Policy
- Cancellation Procedure & Policy
- No-show Policy

Here's a list of everything you need inside your social media bio:

- Quality profile picture
- Identify as a barber
- Your location
- Link to booking site

> **'The customer should know exactly where to book, where you're located, how much you charge, and what kind of services you offer.'**

Run a Smooth Operation

What's a smooth operation? It's a system that is so frictionless you forget you're actually working and the customer feels like they're getting the royal treatment. It should be run so smoothly you no longer have to think about it because it's second nature and automated with technology.

Ask yourself about your system: Does it build trust? Is it consistent? Are you timely? Do you have good appointment flow with little to no interruptions? How can it flow more smoothly?

If you want to have an organized, smooth-running business, you have to structure it a certain way. Get clear and specific on your schedule, breaks, vacations, prices, booking method, cancelation rules, etc., and stick with these details firmly. The structure you build and how well you hold it up will determine what kind of clientele you will have.

People appreciate and like to support businesses that have a clear, predictable, and organized structure. If you try to make everyone happy, you will have a business full of every kind of possible client: cheap clients, walk-in clients, clients with no jobs, clients that are late all the time, ones that try to bribe you to fit them in, clients that want to call for appointments, other ones that want to text you, clients that call every hour to see if anyone canceled, and you will be split in hundred different ways. Suddenly, you won't be able to enjoy the craft you loved, and none of your clients will be happy because they all want and expect different things.

So, set your structure and stick with it. If they don't match, they don't match. Doesn't matter whether they are friends, relatives, or strangers, by doing this early you will avoid a lot of headaches in your business. Trust me.

Work By-Appointment-Only as Soon as Possible

I always recommend to work by-appointment-only, here's why. This allows you to not waste time. It allows you to communicate to your customer that you're constantly busy. It ensures quality and clarity in the booking process.

The Rich Barber knows that it is important to control your time and business. You want to schedule your appointments back to back with pre-set breaks. This allows you to not waste valuable time, and enables you to communicate with your clients that you're consistently busy so it's important that they arrive on time. If they see you sitting around waiting on them, they will subconsciously not value you or your time. I mean, who would?

When I went appointment-only, it angered my friends because they wanted the Chuka that they could text day-of and get an appointment with, and suddenly my business didn't work that way. The ones that respected it stayed and the ones that didn't found a barber that best suited their needs. See, this step is important to complete and stick by because it's tangible and clear. If you're a barber that has been letting your business and clients run you—or one just out of barber college—the messaging to the client is simple: Appointment-only and an automated system is better for them it ensures that they get in and get your best service possible. No interruptions, detailed cut, and booked slot just for them. The system ensures quality!

STAGE 4: WORLD-CLASS SERVICE
PLAY BY PLAY

When you combine your skills and your personality, the result is the experience the customer comes to your barber chair to get. You give them a feeling of increase that allows them to look good and feel better. Once you create an atmosphere with that feeling, whatever you charge your clients, they will continue to pay. Why? Because they feel like they're always getting their money's worth and more. You want them to be excited about coming and feel great leaving.

The goal is to give them a experience that they couldn't get anywhere else.

Treat Them like Royalty

If you treat your customers like royalty, and they will never leave you. Antoine Dunn—a barber at The Rich Barber Hair Studio—has the gift of observation and it gets him tipped generously. It gets pretty hot in Sacramento, and when Dunn sees his client sweating from rushing to the appointment, he will offer him water and a cool towel! It's extra and they love being taken extra special care of. These little things matter.

Anticipate what your client will want or need. If you design this into your business and your behavior, it will become second nature.

> 'The goal is to give
> them a experience
> that they couldn't get
> anywhere else.'

For instance, as they're walking through the door, acknowledge their presence: "Wassup, Mike, I'm going to take care of you in a min, please take a seat and I'll be right with you." Greet them with a smile too, you don't have to be a thug all the time, or Mr. Super Happy; just be flex-able and show character.

This is your friend, your customer, your family; there's a relationship there. Be excited to see them, crack a smile and say wassup!

Then Use the First Five Minutes to Get on the Same Page

When you have a new client in your chair, you should include a consultation with their first haircut. Ask them what they are looking for, and make sure you two are on the same page in regards to the styles they like and the terminology they use.

Nine times out of ten they come to me looking for either a fade or a taper, because that's what I advertise. If it's a fade, then I confirm: "What type of fade? Bald, shadow, high, low?" This way I am clear on what they want.

> 'You know the basics, and as you master the act of barbering, you will be able to see a style clients show you and duplicate them.'

In the age of Instagram, you can always pull out a picture so that you both understand what is being talked about.

There are fade haircuts that get popular online and people will come asking for them. Know them, and have pictures ready so you can confirm what they are looking for.

You know the basics, and as you master the act of barbering, you will be able to see a style clients show you and duplicate them.

Serve Your Lifetime Clients

After you find out how they found out about you, transition into figuring out the kind of cut they came for. Did they see something they liked and now they want it? Or do they want you just to go to work?

Serving your lifetime clients is more than giving a one-of-a-kind cut, it's also about cultivating a deeper relationship with them in your chair. You want to become a part of their team. That's why we emphasize that you should listen twice as much as you talk.

This is your chance to get to know them and create a lasting relationship, one where they want to spend money for your services and your personality. Build a rapport with each new client and they will want to do business with you. People buy from people they like, make them love you!

Maintain a Positive Attitude and Conversation

Positivity attracts positivity. The more positivity you put out, the more you'll get back.

Positivity makes people and your clients want to be around you. I'm not saying you have to be smiling all the time, but it's definitely better to finish strong and positive.

After your done servicing your client, you both should feel good about the time spent.

In general, staying positive will determine all of your experiences in life: your service, the way people talk about you and the people you attract. So don't skip this, it's very important keep a positive mental attitude.

Happily Serve Picky Clients

You might think that having a picky client is a negative thing, but you have got it all wrong. Picky clients are the best, most valuable, and loyal you'll ever have. You want to have reserves of picky and demanding clients. The more special care they need, the more loyal and dependent will become on you and your services.

Work hard to get in tune with your picky customers and understand what makes them feel most confident. Be just as serious about a 360 waver's low taper as he is. These clients will get you to mastery by forcing detail upon you, enjoy each challenge.

Get to know their heads and what makes them look at themselves and think, "I'm fresh. Someone has got to see me today."

Don't ever forget: what you're selling is a feeling! If they get out of your chair and feel like they can take on anything, you've created a lifetime client.

> 'You want to have reserves of picky and demanding clients.'

The Feeling Thermostat

You've got to make sure you're keeping tabs on how you make clients feel.

The feeling is the emergent. It is what you get after a layered experience: it's the feeling you give to the client when they're in your chair, and the feeling they have when they look at themselves in the mirror after they get cut by you.

The feeling is what you want to create during every cut. You want them to feel like a million dollars, like they can go take on the world, get that job they are interviewing for, or ask their girlfriend to marry them.

Think of it is a thermostat and take the client's temperature after every cut. Keep an eye on their behavior when they get up. Are they excited about it? Do they look at themselves differently? If you tackle all of the advice and challenges in this chapter, you will create the feeling every time. Here's a few things you can look out for after every appointment to see how well you did:

- Did they have a positive reaction once you finished?
- Did they use hot key phrases like "I really like it," "this is the best cut I've ever had," "Wow." (Anything that sounds neutral like "it's okay" or "It's cool/good," would not be hot-key phrases)
- Did they smile?

- Did they look at themselves in the mirror and seem genuinely excited about the way they look?
- Did they joyfully pay your price?
- Did they express that they wanted to come back without you asking?
- Did they display gratitude and appreciation?
- Did they display more self confidence on the way out?
- Was there a 'pep' in their step and confidence in movement and posture?
- Did they tip? And if so, how well?

'You've got to make sure you're keeping tabs on how you make clients feel.'

Action Steps:

1. Set up an online booking system.

2. Read the Attractive Personality Habits
   Every Day for 30 Days

3. Set Up Clear Automatic Communication
   (Social Media, Booking System)
   (INFO: Pricing schedule, rules, location)

4. Print out your affirmation and repeat it daily.
   Download it at TheRichBarberMethod.com.

5. Build new habits:
   - Client Acknowledgment & Appointment
     Status Updates
   - New Client Consultations
   - Going the extra mile

MARKETING

The Snowball Effect:

By this point in the book, you understand that every step up the developmental pyramid makes the next step easier. When you have mastered the act of barbering, it makes creating a world-class client experience all the more easy. In the same way, once you have a world-class client experience and give a perfect haircut, marketing is just about documenting and sharing your work on Instagram, social media, and so on.

Focusing on digital marketing and social media is important for barbers, but you need to remember that, in the our industry, word-of-mouth marketing always has and always will be the king. This became clear to me when I worked as a barber in Sacramento. I would be playing basketball with some guys, one would mention he needs a haircut and I'd offer to do it for him. After giving a great experience and a great haircut, he'd recommend me to his friends. Before I knew it, those friends would be telling their friends, family, and colleagues, and in no time, my name was spreading like a wildfire. People would stop seeing their usual barber and switch to me because of how adamantly my clients sold my services.

This snowball effect grows and grows and grows as your clientele grows. Once I mastered the first two domains— The Act of Barbering and Client Experience—then the final domain of Marketing was so much easier. If your

THE MARKETING AFFIRMATION:

" I will promote and market myself to a higher status until my demand is overflowing."

clients leave your chair flying high and feeling fresh, they're going to want to share that experience with their social circles. Word of mouth is powerful, it builds and destroys. Make sure it's working for you and not against you.

You need to think of your clients as walking billboards. They are going to go out into the world and advertise your services. That's is the power behind the combination of mastery and world-class service combined. Did I paint the picture well enough? **CHA-CHING!**

The Higher-Status Mindset

You must promote yourself to a higher status. This process begins with being so great that your clients feel like they have a best-kept secret they must share. No matter what you hear, word of mouth still reigns undefeated. This is because people trust their circle: their friends, family, and associates. Birds of a feather flock together. Your clients love and are loyal to you and your business; their circle wants to get a piece of the plug too.

Through perfecting The Act Of Barbering and your Client Experience, you lay the foundation for promotion, marketing, and the creation of a booming money-making operation. However, promoting yourself to a higher status

> 'My clients felt like a million dollars after being cut by me, and they were walking advertisements in Sacramento.'

is about more than making your name ring bells, it's about creating a strong circle of references and clients that will promote you on your behalf.

My work was on the basketball court, in the gym, in the grocery stores, and at various workplaces. My clients felt like a million dollars after being cut by me, and they were walking advertisements in Sacramento. This put me and my business on another level—a higher status. Once this started happening, any other marketing was like fuel on a fire.

Why Must You Promote Yourself to a Higher Status?

You must make your name ring bells. This means you need to know your value and promote it with confidence.

How do you know your value? You know your value because you've been puttin' in that work, you put in that grind, you're paying your dues, and always going that extra mile. You're working on yourself, you're working on

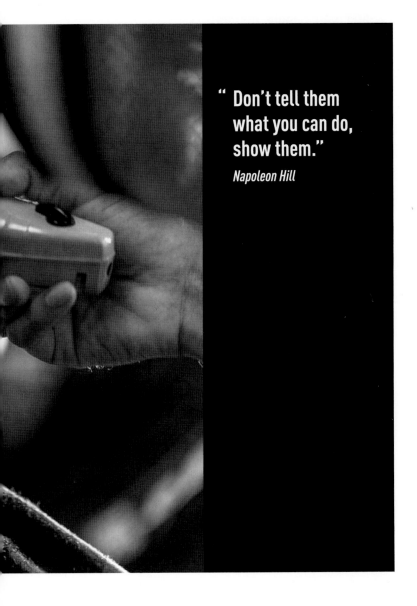

" Don't tell them
what you can do,
show them."

Napoleon Hill

> 'Eventually your content will begin to reach more and more people, just as your current clients will recommend you to more and more people.'

your craft, you have value, you know it, and you show it. The higher status mindset calls for confidence. Confidence when you meet somebody, when they ask you what you do, and when you post on social media. It's all confidence; knowing you have this skill that you've developed and that you're ready to share with the world.

You offer world-class service, don't hesitate to promote it that way. When you've paid your dues, you must make your name ring bells. You have what people need, but if they don't know about you, you can't fulfill their needs. It's not that you're promoting yourself to convince people they need you, they already do, just let them know you're ready to take them on.

Momentum is Key

When it comes to promoting yourself and your services, it is very important that you are persistent regardless of immediate results. You may have some immediate results or you may not, but do it anyway. The goal is to build the habit of promoting and marketing yourself, and then that habit will turn into momentum for your business. Eventually, your content will begin to reach more and more people, just as your current clients will recommend you to more and more people. This is the momentum I am referring to. These days, the snowball effect will happen in person by word of mouth and digitally on social media. It's a continuous chain of reactions.

You can create this chain reaction, you can have momentum work in your favor, but first you must create the momentum. It will not create itself. You have to do it. The faster you can create the momentum the sooner you will increase you demand for you services. Get your name out there, and the fatter your pockets will be when you leave the shop.

> **'Get your name out there, and the fatter your pockets will be when you leave the shop.'**

The Model: From Hunter to Hunted

This is where we create massive demand. This is how we make our name ring bells. Usually, it's better to be the hunter than the hunted, but when it comes to barbering, you don't want to be hunting for clients, you want them to be hunting for you.

There are two parts of Domain Three: Promotion and Marketing. Here's the difference between the two:

Promotion: This is when the act of barbering and the client experience merge together influencing your clients to promote you and your services via word of mouth. You are now at the point that you're doing such a great job, your clients sell your services for you and bring you new business.

Marketing: This is when you take further control of building your personal brand awareness and you blast your work to the masses via social media or any platform that allows the distribution of your content freely or paid.

> 'Blast your work to the masses via social media or any platform.'

STAGE 1: PROMOTION IS PROFICIENCY OF THE FIRST TWO DOMAINS

Once you master your cuts and give world class service, your clients will automatically promote you. The first two domains determine the enthusiasm your clients will have when they leave your shop and go out in the world to promote you. Conquering the first two domains is vital to strong promotion.

It's important for you to breathe life into your business: the haircut and the service. If these don't sell on their own, you won't be promoted. Even worse, if clients are having bad experiences, clients will tell their circles about that too, and it will harm your reputation.

If you follow what was laid down in the previous chapters, then you will be well-developed, your clients will promote you with excitement, and you'll find yourself being hunted down by prospective clients.

Understanding the Customer Journey and Closing Clients

In the beginning, you may not have great data from your social media stats to see exactly where your new clients are coming from. No matter what, nothing is better than real-time data from the new client in your chair. I cannot stress this enough: It is important to ask new clients the powerful question: "How did you hear about me?"

This question gives you insight on how you are being discovered in the community. You will be surprised on the stories new clients share about how they discovered you. These insights help you to keep clients, and attract new ones.

Know where your clients are coming from and ask every time! You will also learn the way people talk about you and sell your services for you to others in their circle. Even if its a walk-in, did they come for you? Or for the shop? How did they find the shop?

It's okay to ask them, and they will often be happy to share.

Know Your Service and How to Close Clients

Whether you grabbed a walk-in or you're servicing a referral, make sure they know you want them to come back—and then make it easy for them!

Some clients don't know that you can re-book with the same barber. This is your chance to educate them. It can be as easy as saying "Hey, if you want to re-book with me, we can book now, or just hit the link in my Instagram bio!"

The Next Two Stages:

In the first two domains of the developmental pyramid, you're the hunter. Those domains are imperative because they lay the strongest foundation to becoming hunted.
I started barbering and built a massive demand for my services before there was Instagram and ways to market and promote online. I did it through the snowball effect of word of mouth.

When you move on to marketing, you no longer wait for others to bring awareness to your developed talent and world class experience, you push it out to the masses yourself.

You make your name ring bells, by displaying your work to your community. This will cause potential clients to discover you and people will begin to hunt you down for your services causing a boom in your demand.

This will up your status and reputation dramatically; it will be then when you will truly understand why it was so important to lay the previous foundation with the two previous domains.

It is here when all domains are operating sumultaneously that you will experience the power of the method, and you will know what it feels like to be the hunted.

STAGE 2: KNOW YOUR VALUE & PROMOTE YOURSELF WITH CONFIDENCE

You're a walking message of who you are and what you do. You've developed something great, now you need to let the world know.

Take it seriously. You're a barber, this is your art, this is your craft. Make sure that whenever anyone comes into contact with your work it attracts. We talked about automated communication, but this is a step further, make sure your bio, photos, videos, and captions also attract. If your ideal client comes in contact with your business, make sure they know you're the barber for them.

I get it: your family, friends etc. follow you, and you're afraid of posting too much, or self-promoting too much. This feeling is real and takes space much like criticism. We are programmed to care what others think and seek

> 'You need to post your best work at least twice a day and your potential customers need to constantly be reminded of what you can offer.'

> # "Know the value of knowing your value."
> *Cleo Wade*

acceptance—I get it. I feel it too. However, our business pages need to be immune to such fuckery. You need to post your best work at least twice a day and your potential customers need to constantly be reminded of what you can offer.

In the beginning, this might mean you're posting your best photos and videos four or five times. It means you're reposting from the @therichbarber Instagram and other inspirational pages so everyone knows you're part of the scene and what styles you're interested in. Your friends and family who are living completely different lives are not going to always understand and support. They might be frustrated with the constant posts and give you grief. Just understand that is normal and take it with a grain of salt. Laugh it off and continue to build the business of your dreams.

STAGE 3: KNOW THE BARBERS PLATFORM & HOW TO USE IT

Instagram is the barber's platform. Yes, if you use other social media platforms, you can still share that content elsewhere.

Instagram has over a billion users and **@barbershopconnect** and many other barber pages show us that millions of people are interested in our billion dollar industry.

Social media is a business tool for The Rich Barber. When you're on Instagram or Snapchat (or any of the other platforms) you promote your business and see what's hot.

What is the trending haircut? Time to master it and showcase how you do it on your social media. Mastering the latest, popular haircuts helps you bring in customers for specific styles. It has been my experience and the experience of the barbers at The Rich Barber Hair Studio that the cuts we post most often are the cuts we service. Do a Klay Thompson taper or an Odell Beckham mohawk and you'll get customers who want that exact cut.

This is how you leverage social media and build your business.

> **'Show potential clients the detail and results that you can bring to the table.'**

The Hunted

To become the hunted, you have to identify what brings you clients and then amplify it.

One of the best way to amplify your skills is to take quality pictures. If the cut is a work of art, take a picture of it. Show potential clients the detail and results that you can bring to the table.

Some Instagram photo ideas include:

- The finished cut
- A before and after side-by-side
- A slideshow of the cut from multiple angles

Make sure to invest in your marketing tools! That means simple video equipment such as a smartphone. I would make sure you have a camera phone that takes clear, quality photos that will capture your detailed work. If you want to take it a step further, invest in a DSLR camera.

Videos take this amplification one step further by perpetuating engagement, they force you to stop and enjoy the journey.

Some Instagram video ideas include:

- If you're going to post a video of an entire cut, don't post one long video. Make sure to edit it like a movie trailer so you're showing the most impressive, exciting parts of the cut. Instagram's built in camera makes it easy to start and stop recording on the same video.
- Make sure to pick a catchy cover photo from the video, such as the before or after of a big transformation.
- Highlight a specific technique or service i.e black mask, the line up, fade etc.

Captions:

Captions should quickly explain what is going on in the content above and also have a call to action. Make sure the most important parts are front loaded because only the first three lines are visible in feeds.

For a photo you might say: "Drop Fade on @ customer's-instagram-handle Book Now #LinkInBio." Or, tell them about the client or what the cut was for: "Got lil' man right for his first day of school Hit the Link in my bio to book," or, "@customer's-instagram-handle has been getting a low taper on his 360 waves since '08. Today, I blessed him with a bald fade. To book with me click the link in my bio." Customers love the story behind the cut.

For a video, you can do something similar, but you need to focus more on engaging them to finish the video: "Transformation cut for @customer's-instagram-handle," or, "Watch this drop fade come together!"

You can always send your customers to your booking link. In the beginning, it will be helpful, and after awhile they will be hunting you down so much you'll want to hide your booking link, or better yet, up your prices! **CHA-CHING! CHA-CHING!**

It's important to identify the name of the haircut so that your client can ask for it, and also show you the picture. You will gain massive amounts of clientele through the use of effective posts. Be clear and showcase your best work.

'Captions should quickly explain what is going on in the content above and also have a call to action.'

Hashtags:

Instagram hashtags allow your work to circulate without someone following you or showing up on their explore page. If a potential client wants a well blended fade, then when they search the hashtag #blurryfade, they'll see results with plenty examples of how you're the hottest #sfbarber.

Hashtag's you should always include:

- #your-name and cuts #TheRichBarberCuts (put this in your bio so that potential customers can see a gallery of your work and follow it)
- #the name of the cut & all variations of it.
- #your city
- #barber
- #therichbarber
- #haircuts
- # your city with barber i.e. #sacbarber for Sacramento or #nybarber for New York

We ran a study that asked: Does Instagram bring you more clientele?

The barbers who were eligible had to be ones who: Posted at least two times a day, had automated communication (refer to page 104 for more), and promoted their barber business first and foremost. We ran the study for three months and had them calculate:

How many total clients they had in that month, how many of those were new clients, and how many of those new clients discovered them from Instagram.

What we found was posting consistent content with clear communication brought more clientele. Every barber found that 85% of their new clientele found them and booked through Instagram.

If you currently have a booking system and post regularly, then you can try this out and conduct your own research. If not, you can start now and in 90 days you will see your growth.

Just pull up your booking schedule from the last three months and document for each month separately:

1. How many total clients did I service?
2. How many of these clients are new?
3. How many of them came from Instagram?

This allows you to see if your demand is increasing, and how many clients are hunting you down through Instagram.

Now that you have the numbers, you can use these to build your marketing.

Identify Your Best Performing Posts & Create Paid Ads from Them

Convert your Instagram profile into business page in your settings tab. This way, you can have the most information available in your analytics. Instagram analytics will show you: who is looking at your feed/story, what people liked and commented, and how much 'reach' you had on the explore page. The reach is so important because it tells you how many new people who don't follow you are looking at your work.

For forteen days after you have posted original content, you can identify the highest performing post and promote it for $2 a day. This allows the platform to put your content in front of more local potential clients. We ran a study with my apprentices Joel & Julio which took their best performing picture and best performing video in intervals of seven days and promoted it. The variables we used to identify the best performing posts were website clicks and engagement. This allowed their most engaging posts to work with them locally, and target a certain demographic, and generated on average two more clients a week on top of what they usually generate from organic postings.

This data tells us to never rely solely on paid marketing, because organic posts and content is still where the real power is. It gets you into the habit of consistently creating content and sharing your work, and the promoted posts are an added layer to your overall marketing.

Action Steps:

1. Make your Instagram account a business page.

2. Make sure your Instagram profile photo attracts and you have automated communication in your bio.

3. Establish service awareness online on platforms like Yelp, Google business etc.

4. Fill Out the Creative Content Guide at TheRichBarberMethod.com.

5. Print out your affirmation and repeat it daily.

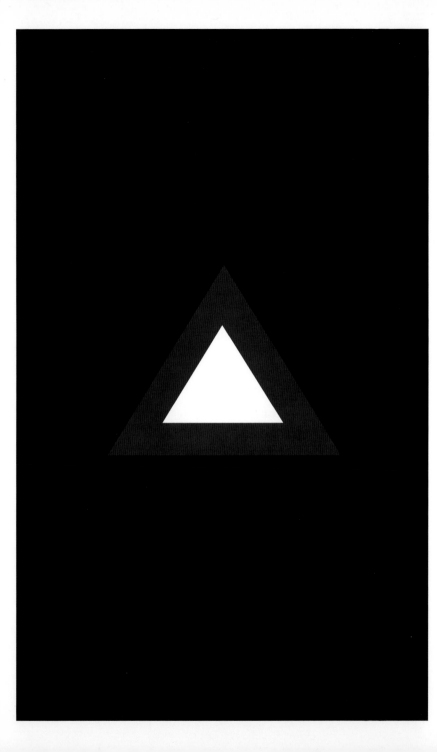

THE PINNACLE:

TIME TO UP YOUR PRICE/ CHARGE MORE

The Rich Barber®

Most barbers plateau or burn out because they never had a clue how to build a strong foundation for their business. They just jumped into barbering and started cutting hair, accepted anything that came their way, and bent over backwards to keep clients happy.

I get it: when you have no idea or model with which to navigate the barber game, you get desperate and start to hurry. I know because I did it. I'm not saying that this doesn't work or that it can't work for a while. what I'm saying is that it's not sustainable nor smart and most profitable.

If you are good at what you do you and you don't have a method with which to continually analyze and adjust your business structure and price based on your market value, your income will eventually plateau or your will burnout from overworking and stress.

Before The Rich Barber Method, barbers wouldn't let systems and technology go to work for them; they would try to be everything in their business and serve everybody. And we all know that little or no clientele equals little or no money.

By this point, you have gone through and gained proficiency of the domains. You have taken on the mindsets, done the work, and have moved up the developmental ladder. You have gone from attracting clients to keeping them. Now you need to charge more.

Can I Raise My Prices Now?: How To Move Up The Pyramid

Once you've gotten a customer, you want to keep them. Until a barber has mastered the three domains of The Rich Barber Method and is using them in combination, it will be difficult to get a customer you can retain in the first place. It shouldn't take more effort to get a new client and then win them over than it does to keep the ones you have now.

How much do you want it? If you kind of want it, then you most likely won't get it. But if there is a fire in you, then you can get it. Either way, you will have a burning desire to get it once you've completed this book and taken all the actions. If you haven't taken any shortcuts, if you've taken all the action steps, if you've been doing your affirmations, and improving your skills in all the domains, then moving up the developmental model is inevitable.

If you do what you've been taught, they will pay. When your demand begins to outweigh your availability, use the Up Your Price Analysis.

The Up Your Price Analysis

The Up Your Price Analysis was created to help you scale your business intelligently, fairly, and with confidence based on your current demand. The Up Your Price Analysis will help you figure out which price is best to maximize revenue, and how to raise your price without causing any negative impact on your income. The analysis will allow you to see if you can charge more without making less.

I am aware of other factors that affect each barber individually, but analysis projects numbers and is unable to take this into consideration. This is a simple, effective approach that allows the barber to make a decision through data and provides a method instead of purely guesswork.

There was a time in my barber career when I understood that I could charge more, work less, and keep the same income. And if I decided to work the same amount of hours per day after raising my prices, then I would obviously make more money.

This is why it's so important to master The Rich Barber Method: by doing this you can create a massive flow of demand that will allow to have more choices. The bigger the demand the better. Below is a example of how the Up Your Price Analysis works. In the first column you have three different scenarios. You have your (1) Original Price,

(2) New Price when you cut less/or lose 25% of clients, and you have (3) New Price Scenario when you cut the same amount after upping your prices. Then along each of the rows you have how much income you make per day, per week, and per month based on the number cuts you do per day for each scenario.

	SCENARIO	PRICE PER HAIRCUT	HAIRCUTS PER DAY	INCOME PER WEEK (5 DAYS)	INCOME PER MONTH (20 DAYS)
(1)	Original Price	$25 Per Haircut	8	$1,000	$4,000
(2)	New Price (Less # of Cuts Per Day)	$35 Per Haircut	6	$1,050	$4,200
(3)	New Price (Same # of Cuts Per Day)	$35 Per Haircut	8	$1,400	$5,600

You can see that there is no decrease in income in the example on the previous page. When you follow the method, you can use the Up You Price Analysis to up your prices based on your demand and see three scenarios that give you a accurate idea of what to expect, giving you the confidence you need to make the decision to up your price. If you have a 80-90% occupancy rate in your schedule, you most likely will be in the second senecio when you up your price, but will gradually end up closer to the third scenario once you fill the freed up available time with new clients who pay your new price. But if you occupancy rate is 95% and above with overflow of clientele, then you can immediately experience a leap straight to the third scenario. Also, remember the snowball effect is still working in your favor, bringing you more and more demand for your services if you've followed the instructions in each domain. Visit TheRichBarberMethod.com for access to the Up Your Price Analysis and more information on how to use it.

You must realize that a barber is a single individual with limited amount of energy and time, and not a product that can be duplicated and multiplied. At a certain point, a barber must look at their time and energy as the supply (thing being sold), and not service itself. Had I understood this and applied it earlier I would have reduced the amount of frustration, confusion, and stress cause by not having a strategic plan in place for when my demand grew exceptionally. But once I understood and applied

> 'You must realize that a barber is a single individual with limited amount of energy and time.'

a strategic plan, I regained control of my business and fulfillment with barbering.

The Up Your Price Analysis—which is based on the economic law of supply and demand—should be used to raise your prices only when you have built a consistent flow of clientele based on the foundation of The Rich Barber Method.

The law of supply and demand says that there is an inverse relationship between price and demand: as price increases, demand decreases, and vice versa. To make this plain and simple, the law of supply and demand goes like this: When something is available in large quantities the price tends to go down, which causes more people to buy more of it. When the price goes up, it causes people to buy less of it.

To say it a different way: People tend to place more value on things that are rare and high quality.

Sometimes it's nature that provides the supply, and sometimes it's people. This is why flawless diamonds cost more than others. The same goes for beachfront real estate, by nature there is a limited supply. But then you hear of a wealthy individual who spends $110 million at an auction for a single Basquiat painting. It was one man's expertise, and the rareness of his work, which was able to bring his demand so high that his work was worth insane prices.

As for us barbers, there is a limitless supply available. Remember that at the beginning of this book I quoted Forbes saying that barbering was the fastest growing profession in the US in 2017. Therefore, if you want to have the ability to charge more than average, you must create this circumstance. Your demand and value will never naturally go up because there is no lack of supply of barbers. The barber industry is hot, you've got to stand out.

You should now see clearly why it is so important to follow everything laid down in this book in order to become one who stands out amongst the crowd: You can be the one who is in high demand despite all the options available all around you.

A Labor of Love

There is another equally important component which relates to upping your price. It has been my experience that as a barber grows in demand, they are better able to keep the enjoyment and fulfillment that they get at work because the compensation for their services are in line with their perceived value. If a barber is in high demand and knows that he can make more money, but settles for less, it cause a imbalance with him and his labor of love. That's why it's important for your price to grow along with you and your demand.

Whenever you use the Up Your Price Analysis, your weekly and monthly revenue should be consistent and predictable with demand steadily growing. If you are practicing The Rich Barber Method, you already know that this not meant to be used as a way to cheat those who we serve in any way.

You know that you must be worth the price you charge, and that you must always do your best to deliver value to those who you serve. The idea is that you will price yourself according to the value you bring to the marketplace based on the demand you experience for your services.

The Up Your Price Analysis is used to keep that balance and equilibrium between the barber and his clients so that it is always a win-win situation. It's important to know that as you up your price, there will be those clients who you have out-priced, and that is okay. If you're following all the steps of The Rich Barber Method, you'll be able to up your price, maybe lose some clients who can't afford you anymore, while still make the same amount of money, or ideally more.

Just make sure that the time when you did service them, you gave it all you had. As you grow, that will be what matters: the love, appreciation, and respect of your clients. Growth can be tough sometimes because of the relationships we build, but it always feels good to know that there is no hurt feelings from your past clients. If done right, there will only be respect from them.

If you do as this book says, and fully embrace and adopt The Rich Barber Method and mindset there will come a time when you will have built a personal brand that people feel is valuable and unique in its own way.

"The barber life is so much better when you're in demand, making money, and winning. Trust Me!"

Chuka The Barber

Action Steps:

Use the Up Your Price Analysis when you're at least 80-90% booked with increasing demand. For optimal results preferably 95-100% with overflow.

Communicate The Price Increase:
When you've decided to charge more you should:

1. Give at least a 14 day notice of service price increase and a general announcement via social media, mass email, or mass text.

   The first thing I do when I increase prices is say thank you to my clients. I sincerely express my appreciation for their support and loyalty and then I'm transparent with them about why it is time to raise my prices. The strategy for effectively communicating your price increase to clients is to relay the message:

" **Because there has been substantial increase in the demand for my services, I have to raise my prices.**"

You don't want to leave a negative feeling, you just want to be confident in charging what your worth. You can explain, but don't apologize. Often, your best clients will be surprised that you didn't raise your prices sooner because they value your work.

2. Reflect price change in all automated communication: booking app, social media bio, etc. Here is a price transition example:

Haircut - $30
New Price $40 Starting January 1, 2019

3. Build crazy demand, up your price, & REPEAT!

OUTRO

The most pivotal moment in my career happened years ago when I took the leap of faith and made the decision to go after my dreams. When I think back about that decision, it always seems to paralyze me for a moment, because I know that things would not be as great as they are for me today if it wasn't for this decision. The decision was to go after my dreams. To take on the identity of The Rich Barber and manifest that shit.

You picked up this book and read up to this point, and chances are that you picked it up because you yourself are at a pivotal point in your life or career. A decision to go for it at this very moment could be the major turning point of your life.

The Rich Barber Method is the most fundamental, simple, and workable model I could possibly create to give barbers the ability to consistently attract clients, keep them, and charge more.

The principles within the model are no invention of mine own, but come from years of experience and studying the greats. What I did was test the knowledge and then organize it in such a way that it can be utilized to achieve success by us barbers.

At first, you may not understand why and how these principles work in your favor, but when applied properly over time, it works. I challenge you to just test it. Really follow it and put forth the effort everyday for at least 30 days and then decide if your life and business has gotten better or worse.

If you're not prepared to try it, ask yourself why? Is it fear? Is it because you'd rather be doing something other than barbering? Or is it because you don't want to work hard? Procrastination is one of the greatest enemies of those who desire success. Speed of implementation is a quality of the successful. Do the second, kill the first. Set all distractions aside. Begin now, and start implementing all that you read if you haven't been already. If you have already begun implementing, then you're well on you way.

In the first 21 years of my life, I probably only read one complete book. Who would have ever thought I'd be writing a book based on a business model for barbers that I have tested in my own life while building a multi-million dollar company? I was raised in poverty, supported on government welfare, grew up without a father, caught a felony that ended my basketball career when I was 20, and failed many business ventures along the way.

I've had almost every reason to quit, settle for less and justify it with legitimate reasons. How was I able to achieve what I have achieved today? I never quit and always decided to keep going despite all obstacles, and of course, by applying the principles that are in this book.

You have to do it, no one can do it for you. But now you have a guide that will work for you if you use it.

Money is not to be sought directly, but comes as a result of doing certain things in a certain way. Study and apply this book until you reach your goals. Go to the links I set up and access the tools that go along with the book, and stay connected with me and The Rich Barber pages through YouTube, Facebook, and Instagram so that you can stay inspired and motivated throughout your journey to the top. This is the life I've always wanted, and I truly believe that if you put in the work, you can have yours to.

So let me ask you this question again: What if a simple, straightforward idea could lift you out of your current position and up to a level where you have control over your career and destiny? What if this simple idea could spark new life and action in you, opening up a world of opportunity?

Would you take on this idea? There will be thousands of Rich Barbers worldwide.

The big question is: **Will you be one of them?**

"Leave the world alone, and change the concept of yourself."

Neville

ACKNOWLEDGEMENTS

To the all the barbers worldwide who have made this industry what it is today, and made The Rich Barber Movement possible. To my mother for shaping who I am today with her love, strength, and courage she displayed despite all adversity. Thank you to my brother Jovon who always believed in me and supported me from day one. Thanks to my sister Keziah and brother Chidi for your love and support through some of my toughest times. Thank you to my daughter's wonderful mother Aaliyah, I appreciate you so much. To my father in law (Pops) Arthur Swift who believed in me and gave the $500 downpayment I needed to start barber college. Thanks to my second mom, Debra Brown, and the whole Brown family who showed me a different side of life and whose love and support has been unconditional. Thanks to my friend and mentor Chris Johnson whose inspiration and guidance has been immeasurable. To my friend and mentor Scott Syphax whose life experience and wisdom continues to shed light on life, bringing understanding and growth my character.

To my friend and mentor Ramesh Lochan who introduced me to the power of The Law of Success. To my friend Calvin Anderson who encouraged me to become a barber and has always supported me throughout my barber career. To my friends Tej & Damon Baath who masterminded with me every week at the Peet's Coffee on 20th & J during the birth of The Rich Barber. To Shantelle Johnson who saw the possibilities early on even though when she came to work with me the business was run out of the hallway of my apartment. To Madyson Baker-Jones for your unwavering belief in me and the vision, and your help communicating that vision to the industry, and helping bring this book to life. And to the late Napoleon Hill whose life work contributed tremendously to my success but more importantly to my self-discovery and growth that goes beyond things of a material nature.

God is the greatest.

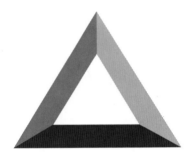